D0842664

916.6043 CEL

Celati, Gianni, 1937-

Adventures in Africa /

3/01 c2000.

DISCARDED

11/01   8/02 @ CAP (3)   1/04 (6)
3

SANTA CRUZ PUBLIC LIBRARY

SANTA CRUZ, CALIFORNIA 95060

ADVENTURES IN AFRICA

ADVENTURES IN
AFRICA

GIANNI CELATI

TRANSLATED BY ADRIA BERNARDI
FOREWORD BY REBECCA WEST

THE UNIVERSITY OF CHICAGO PRESS ◉ CHICAGO AND LONDON

SANTA CRUZ PUBLIC LIBRARY
Santa Cruz California

GIANNI CELATI is an Italian writer living in Brighton, England. *Avventure in Africa,* his tenth book, won the first Zerilli-Marimó Prize awarded by New York University's Casa Italiana and the Bellonci Foundation in Italy in 1998.

ADRIA BERNARDI is author of *The Day Laid on the Altar* and *In the Gathering Woods* and translator of Tonino Guerra's *Abandoned Places.*

Originally published as *Avventure in Africa,* © 1998 Giangiacomo Feltrinelli Editore Milano

The University of Chicago Press, Chicago 60637
The University of Chicago Press, Ltd., London
© 2000 by The University of Chicago
All rights reserved. Published 2000
Printed in the United States of America
09 08 07 06 05 04 03 02 01 00   1 2 3 4 5

ISBN: 0-226-09955-5 (cloth)

Library of Congress Cataloging-in-Publication Data

Celati, Gianni, 1937–
    [Avventure in Africa. English]
    Adventures in Africa / Gianni Celati
        p. cm.
    ISBN 0-226-09955-5 (alk. paper)
    1. Mali—Description and travel. 2. Mauritania—Description and travel. 3. Senegal—Description and travel. 4. Celati, Gianni, 1937-—Journeys—Mali. 5. Celati, Gianni, 1937-—Journeys—Mauritania. 6. Celati, Gianni, 1937-—Journeys—Senegal. I. Title

    DT551.27.C4513 2000
    916.604'33—dc21   00-029931
                                                            CIP

♾ The paper used in this publication meets the minimum requirements of the American National Standard for Information Sciences— Permanence of Paper for Printed Library Materials, ANSI Z39.48-1992.

FOREWORD

Gianni Celati, born in the town of Sondrio in northern Italy in 1937, is a fiction writer, critic, and translator. He studied at the University of Bologna where he wrote a thesis on James Joyce; he then took up a teaching post in the department of Anglo-American literature and spent over two decades in Bologna, so that he is often thought of as a native son of that university city and of the region of Emilia-Romagna where many of his short stories of the 1990s are set. In fact, his family ties to the region are strong; his mother's family came from the area around Ferrara, and Celati has returned in recent years to peripatetic investigations of and writings on the Po Valley. He began publishing critical and theoretical essays in the mid-1960s in the context of the then vigorous debates on literature that Italian neoavant-garde intellectuals had stimulated. Having exhausted the vein of neorealist fiction that flourished in the decade or more after World War II, Italian writers were looking for new forms and contents that might invigorate narrative and poetry alike. Italo Calvino, Umberto Eco, and many others took part in the theoretical and practical work of this period, and Celati added his critical (and, in the 1970s, his creative) voice to the ferment of ideas with deeply thoughtful essays on Joyce, Céline, Bakhtin, structuralism, orality, archeological approaches to knowledge, and many other salient topics of the 1960s, when the shift from modernity to postmodernity was emergent. These essays collectively form a sustained critique of institutional forms of literature and reveal Celati's long-standing preference for oral culture, marginal figures, and "everyday" stories.

Italo Calvino wrote the introduction to Celati's first published fictional work, the 1971 *Comiche* (Slapstick silent films), which appeared in the Einaudi series oriented to experimental writing by young and generally unknown authors. Calvino was to remain Celati's friend and collaborator until the former's death in 1985. In the 1970s Celati also pursued his interest in literary translation, publishing Italian versions of works by Swift, Barthes, Gerhardie, Céline, and others. A collection of his critical essays appeared in 1975 with the title *Finzioni occidentali: Fabulazione, comicità e scrittura* (Western fictions: Fabulation, comicality, and writing). Meanwhile, Celati continued to write fiction, and three works were published in the 1970s: *Le avventure di Guizzardi* (The adventures of Guizzardi, 1973); *La banda dei sospiri* (The gang [or soundtrack] of sighs, 1976); and *Lunario del paradiso* (Paradise almanac, 1978). Later described by their author as a trilogy made up of "everyday tales," these three books, with a completely rewritten version of *Lunario del paradiso*, were brought together into one volume entitled *Parlamenti buffi* (Funny chatter) in 1989. While *Comiche* is written in the estranged voice of a paranoid, perhaps completely insane, poor lost soul, *La banda dei sospiri* and *Lunario del paradiso* are semi-autobiographical tales of, respectively, an adolescent and a young man who seek to make their way in a world dominated by repressive families and frightening authority figures; both books reflect the rebellious mood of the late 1960s and precede by more than two decades the recent trend in Italy of youth-oriented fiction. All of these fictional writings of the 1970s show Celati at his most linguistically experimental, varying as they do from the unbalanced ravings of *Comiche*'s protagonist, to the comically grotesque ungrammatical speech of Guizzardi, to the colloquial, spoken style of the latter two books. They are also marked by Celati's preference for loosely structured plots more akin to those of the romance than of the traditional realist novel; events follow events in the casual and even illogical way of desultory, quotidian experience rather than according to some predetermined and tightly controlled line. These early fictions all show, to one degree or another, Celati's interest in finding alternatives to the well-wrought realist novel and his love for extra-literary models such as the spoken word, the embodied comedy of silent film stars such as Buster Keaton and Charlie Chaplin, and the common "adventures" and misadventures of family life.

The Italian critical establishment recognized Celati's original new voice, and he was awarded the coveted Bagutta literary prize in 1974 for *Le avventure di Guizzardi,* the book among his early works that has best stood the test of time, remaining one of the few fictional works to have emerged out of the period of experimentalism in Italy that are still read and appreciated today. Nonetheless, by the late 1970s Celati felt the need to withdraw from the literary scene to rethink his approach to writing, and he published only essays and translations from the appearance in 1978 of *Lunario del paradiso* until 1985, when he once more entered the mainstream publishing world with a highly successful collection of stories, *Narratori delle pianure* (translated as *Voices from the Plains*). A departure from his earlier penchant for experimental and often comic writing, the volume is made up of short tales written in pared-down, minimalist prose. They recount the common (if often blackly humorous or hauntingly sad) stories of contemporary people living in the small towns that dot the Po Valley, the flat and unexceptional landscape of which becomes a running metaphor for Celati's poetics of unpretentiousness. These stories capture something of the particularly compelling qualities of the Po Valley that can be seen as well in certain groundbreaking films set in that landscape, such as Visconti's *Ossessione* or Antonioni's *Il deserto rosso:* the utter flatness, the lack of known monuments, the obfuscating fog. People live their lives, and their stories, without benefit of spatial—and, it is implied, philosophical—points of elevation or domination that might serve to transcend the muddle of life; all is close to the horizon, and often enveloped in the misty, watery Po landscapes, which represent the basic mystery of quotidian life. How storytelling can help us to find order, compassion for others, and even comfort in the face of a progressively more mysterious and complex postmodern existence is now central to Celati's work of this period, which was heavily influenced by his collaboration with the distinguished Po Valley photographer Luigi Ghirri. Always a great peripatetic, Celati literally found his stories while on the road with Ghirri, by observing, listening, and attuning himself to the endless supply of narratives out there for the taking.

Since the publication of *Narratori delle pianure,* Celati has continued to write fiction and what he calls "reportage" or "tales of observation," the latter category one in which *Avventure in Africa* can rightly be placed. Nor has his work as a translator ceased; in 1991 his Italian version of Melville's "Bartleby the Scrivener" appeared, as well as versions of Jack London's *The Call of the Wild* and Stendhal's *La Chartreuse de Parme.* Among other activities of the last decade are Celati's co-founding and co-editing of the literary journal *Il Semplice* and the direction of two video films, *Strada provinciale delle anime* (Provincial road of souls) and *Il mondo di Luigi Ghirri* (The world of Luigi Ghirri), the former a visual exploration of the same Po Valley towns and landscapes in which his recent short stories are set, and the latter a homage to the late photographer with whom he so profitably collaborated while exploring that ambience. Celati has also returned to his early interest in orality and performance with his prose version of Renaissance epic poet Boiardo's *Orlando innamorato* and his theatrical piece *Recita dell'attore Vecchiatto nel teatro di Rio Saliceto* (Performance of the actor Vecchiatto in the theater of Rio Saliceto), both of which the writer has "performed" in many public readings in Europe and the United States. The restless critical and creative research by which Celati's work is marked shows no sign of ending, as he goes on traveling and searching for what he has called "fictions in which to believe."

Celati's interest in writing "anti-monumental" fiction—stories, that is, which remain rooted in unexceptional lived experience—informs *Adventures in Africa* as well as his earlier work. The book is organized into a series of "notebooks" that were written while on the road in West Africa (Senegal, Mali, and Mauritania). Celati made the trip with a filmmaker friend, Jean Talon, who had decided to go to West Africa to develop a documentary on native healers. Celati, who has traveled extensively throughout Europe and the United States, went along on the trip, perhaps motivated by nothing other than his sustained wanderlust. It is possible, however, that he was looking to find again what he has called a "state of self-forgetfulness" in which he believes is produced the best writing. Walter Benjamin, one of Celati's obvious sources for ideas about storytelling, wrote of "the most perfect fusion of the involuntary, and supreme intention" to be found in Robert Walser's writing, as well as of Schiller's concept of grace as "the union of the voluntary and the involuntary." Celati subscribes to this conception of writing, wherein the writer puts self aside and instead enters into externality and otherness. In his earlier book of "adventures," *Le avventure di Guizzardi,* he had succeeded in entering into the flow and sound of his odd protagonist's voice; perhaps the title of *Adventures in Africa* echoes the earlier one because the writer believes that he has succeeded in recapturing the "grace" that fueled Guizzardi's story, albeit in a plain, spoken style that is light-years away from the highly constructed language of the 1973 work. *Adventures in Africa* is an "adventure" in a kind of writing that is freed of literary artifice and self-oriented expressiveness both. As disorganized and undisciplined as the trip itself turned out to be, the record of it, now shaped into this book, is the end result of a writerly discipline practiced over the last three decades, which has led to what Celati himself called in a recent interview "a state of grace."

The term "adventure" signifies etymologically "what will come in the future." The surprising nature of unknown future events is precisely what drives the narrative line of *Adventures in*

Africa, for the planned goal of the trip—the filming of a documentary—is never reached. What in fact occurs is a comedy of errors, delays, misinformation, and wandering about, as contacts are unfindable, means of transportation are unreliable, and complications arise at every turn. If the book is in part an "adventure" in a kind of writing, it is, however, also a record of actual events, places, people, and encounters that add up to a portrait of the West African countries visited. We come to understand how economically poor the people are, how arid the desert landscapes are, how dependent the urban populations are on tourism for their daily sustenance. In fact, one of the most amusing and appealing aspects of the book is its "ethnography" of tourists, who have come to form a virtually distinct "ethnic group." Tourists' behavior, appearance, and speech are all carefully (and humorously) recorded by Celati, who includes himself and his traveling companion in this ultimately risible "tribe." There is no linear plot to this book, then; it instead follows the zigzagging lines and circles both of the errant trip itself and of Celati's always intense and original observations.

Because *Adventures in Africa* is characterized by a wonderfully flowing momentum, sustained by the endless diversity of sights, experiences, and people offered up to Celati as he moves always toward new, future "things to come," it would not do to dissect it into salient themes or "messages" to the reader. I therefore simply wish to highlight some recurrent elements that run throughout the book and aid in shaping it into a "story of observation" rather than merely a series of unconnected jottings. First, there is the topic of writing itself. Celati often refers to the act of writing on the road: on a bus; seated under a tree while waiting for his friend Talon, who is always searching for the next Coca-Cola, which he drinks with industrial-strength passion; in a train compartment where the writer fascinates a young African woman who becomes a friend and reappears several times in the book. There are references to the interest his ceaseless writing stimulates in observers, who want to know what he is doing and why; who he is; if he is "famous" back in Europe. Moreover,

Celati elaborates a sort of parallel narrative concerning the adventures in Africa of a pair of fictional friends named Cevenini and Ridolfi. The old Italians, from a small provincial town, decide to travel to West Africa to find a cure by African healers for Ridolfi's fits of insanity, during which he would periodically smash all the furniture in his home. Writing is never far from Celati's mind, and he is clearly already filtering and framing his experiences in words as he goes through them. Because much of the book we now have is recounted in the present tense, the events of the trip and the text itself are practically coterminous, thus creating a strong sense for the reader of immediacy and immersion: a kind of "you are there" quality that adds greatly to the appeal of the book. It is as if we readers are carrying on a running "conversation" with Celati as he makes observations, ruminates on diverse topics, and fantasizes, always in a narrative voice that is as close to a spoken voice as possible.

As I have mentioned, tourists are another recurrent topic. In West Africa, they stand out as a minority of "wealthy" whites in a world of "poor" blacks. Celati notes that many Western tourists react to their uncomfortable minority status by retreating into the fancy, air-conditioned hotels that the writer calls "concentration camps for tourists." Therein, everything is controlled, regulated, clean, and protected from the chaotic foreignness outside. Celati prefers instead to immerse himself in the disorganized daily commerce surrounding him, which consists of the African vendors' attempts to sell trinkets to any and all tourists, as well as of chatting, wandering about, and having all sorts of unexpected encounters. The tourists' orchestrated experiences seem to him coldly ceremonial and false, while the apparent aimlessness of much that goes on in the streets gives rise often to living exchanges between two "others": the white Italian tourist, who is "other" to the native populace, and the black people whose countries these are, and who are "other" to Celati. His preference for "commerce" of the seemingly disorganized African kind, which is akin to "chatting" and "friendly agreement as if in a family setting," is, of course, a critique of the

Western capitalistic "passion for business" that is motivated by economics alone. On the trip home, Celati and Talon have a stopover in Paris where everything is clean, ordered, new, and up to date. In this "perpetual documentary" of Western postmodern abundance, Celati misses the "nothing" he has glimpsed in West Africa, that "nothing that cannot be bought . . . the nothing of the sky and the universe, or the nothing that the others have who do not have anything." Travel has become a way of shedding possessions, self, pretensions, and preconceptions; writing is a light trace of the blessed "nothing" that remains.

In conclusion, I want to thank Adria Bernardi, and the University of Chicago Press, for taking on the translation of *Avventure in Africa*. As someone who has written on Celati's fiction for many years, I am personally delighted to see the appearance of this book in English, for it serves to introduce one of contemporary Italy's most original writers to a new audience of readers. Stories such as his remind us that we all have tales to recount and that, by telling and listening to everyday narratives, we share our human state, made up as it is of abounding "adventures" or "what comes next," whether in West Africa, Italy, or Chicago, Illinois.

Rebecca West

NOTE

In January 1997, I accompanied Jean Talon on a journey
to West Africa that took us from Mali to Senegal and
Mauritania. Initially, it was going to be a trip researching the
possibility of making a documentary about the healing methods
used by Dogon healers, who are employed at the Center for Traditional Medicine in Bandiagara, which is located in the high-
lands of Mali.

I publish the journals of the trip as I wrote them along the
way, with revisions and adjustments to make them readable.
They are dedicated to the friends who want to know where we
have been and to the friends whom we met.

FIRST NOTEBOOK

1 Yesterday, arriving at the airport in Bamako, at 2:30 in the morning, I stopped understanding what was happening. Confusion began as soon as we passed through the hands of the customs officials. An old man with a long blue tunic, a Coptic cap, a withered body, his skin pearly gray, latched on to me at the exit. He was talking about a *navette,* the shuttle minibus going to Bamako. All around there were boys pulling me by the arms, others asking me what my name was. There was a buzzing in my ears, and so, confused and half-deaf, I told the old man we would take his minibus. The boy Moussa immediately sprang into action as the associate of the old man and said that in order to retrieve the baggage, he needed the baggage claim ticket. What do I know about the customs in this country? I didn't even know where my traveling companion had ended up in the tumult of people crowded inside this big room that looks like a barracks. In any case, when the bags were retrieved and then when the boy Moussa pushed us onto the bus of the old gray man, I understood that now our lives nearly depended on them. Dragged across the space, as if in dreams and storms, I saw Moussa fending off many boys who were running after us trying to grab hold. He had gotten there first, and he had first claim on us. Later, on the minibus, he was offended that I'd forgotten his name already. I tried to win his sympathy by explaining that there's a buzzing in my ears that goes on all the time and it causes me to miss many sounds, but nothing doing. I could have retrieved the baggage perfectly well myself, there were no formalities for baggage claims, except for the fact that everyone was elbowing his way forward to grab at enormous cartons or enormous suitcases, or else sacks of rice, or wrapped-up pipes, or spare tires, even a crate containing three live chickens that had been carried by plane from Paris. Naturally, everyone was speaking a language that I do not understand, but in any case, I understand almost nothing here, and I don't even know what I came to do in Africa.

On the way to Bamako, I saw only red earth in the headlights, the streets full of potholes as if they had been bombed. The minibus bumped along like a plane in an air pocket. Then there were long rows of tiny houses, for the most part shacks, or lean-to roofs covered with straw; the doors of the little shops were shut, and above the doors in the dark were those little white neon tubes like the kind used in Italy after the war. Every hut or little house had an air of a soul lost on the savanna, each with its small fairy tale-like flicker, a neon tube of colorless and particle-filled light. As for the rest, I was deafened by Moussa, who every two minutes would ask me if I was all right, me replying yes, but becoming less and less convinced of it. I tried to tell him we needed a hotel, but he kept asking me questions about Italy, he wanted to know if I knew a certain Armando, who was a tailor by profession. Only later did it occur to me that he was speaking about the famous couturier Armani.

2   In order not to consider myself on vacation, I have to write every day, as if I were at home, so therefore working as usual, but temporarily dislocated to a concentration camp for tourists. We are in a hotel named the Hôtel de l'Amitié, and I ask myself what kind of amity we're talking about. One understands at once that the tourists have sequestered themselves and have no desire whatsoever to speak with each other or to see one another. In the elevator, they don't know where to look, to make friends seems to be prohibited. This hotel must have been built during the period of Mali's socialist regime, and Jean says that it looks like many of the high-rise buildings one sees in Moscow. From its appearance, which is like a gigantic beehive, he knows without a doubt it's Soviet, like other things seen during our walks, starting with the police. According to Jean, even the prostitutes hidden in the shadows in the bar know what Soviet means; they strike the same poses as the prostitutes in the state-run hotels in Russia . . . But more than anything, we are totally unprepared for the fact of being white. Because here we are representing not that which we are, or believe ourselves to be, but that which we're supposed to be (rich, powerful, modern, consumers of everything). And we carry around this representation as if it were a spacesuit, everyone in his own suit, which isolates him from the external world. For Jean, it's become almost a fixation, and as soon as he sees some tourists, he starts repeating to me a word he has invented: "Look at the white *pingoni,* that's how we are." He has even discovered that the rule of the *pingoni* is to pretend not to see each other when they pass on the street, exactly the way the guests of the Hôtel de l'Amitié do.

3 Bamako is an enormous village cut by streets laid out like a chessboard, invaded by red sand that the desert wind spreads everywhere, with an administrative center where all the state offices are, and dilapidated neighborhoods all around here and there along the Niger. The sidewalks along the main street in front of the hotel are full of vendors selling statuettes, and they quickly eyeball you, determining whether you are someone not yet in the know, or whether you're already an expert on the subject of buying. They have lightning-glances, Jean says. If you aren't yet in the know, they call out to you, as if to a childhood friend, otherwise they don't even bother to look at you. Stick-thin trees along the sidewalks, straw canopies filled with statuettes and other items for tourists, a flabby woman with a beautiful azure veil, a man without legs who drags himself along on his wrists, a cigarette vendor sitting on the ground with a little table, many cyclists in an intersection where there's a garden with a bust done in the civic style. Then we are on the street with the banks, where I can't see anything anymore because every square meter is filled with so much stuff. Fruit vendors, lottery booths, blind singers, tires, scrap metal, old motorbikes, buckets filled with small nuts, bananas gone a little bad, live and dead chickens, heaps of indistinguishable merchandise, dust and garbage, black and white and albino humanity. Among other things, I'm also deaf and dazed from the continuous buzzing in my ears, but if I could, I would try to make note of everything.

4 The hotel exit. Like being completely at the mercy of others, above all, because of the aftermath of our encounter with Moussa. I paid this Moussa 2000 CFA, as a way of being rid of his services, but at the hotel's exit, a day later, a small gang of his emissaries surround us. The head of this gang is a boy with a maimed arm and the face of a thug, Mohammed, sixteen years old, who, already knowing that it's our intention to go to the Dogon country, introduced himself as an authentic Dogon. I don't know how to ascertain if this is so, except for the fact that he is a formidable talker and all these doubts make me have confidence in him. He never went to school, he learned French on the street, he speaks the Dogon dialects, and Bambara, and Peul, and others as well, he says. Certainly he is not timid, and each time my eyes wander away from him, he takes it as an opportunity to offer his services, such that walking around on the streets I must try to look around me as little as possible. Boys in his gang follow behind, easily keeping up with my marathon-runner's stride, my only weapon in opposing Mohammed's rhetoric. It's like this from the moment we set foot outside the Hôtel de l'Amitié. Still dizzy from the night before at the Hôtel Dakan, with no sleep because of the mosquitoes.

5 It came back to me, how Moussa introduced himself to us on the bus. He showed us his documents as an authorized tourist guide, consisting of a sheet of notebook paper, handwritten, contained within a plastic sheath. Then the nocturnal saraband began once we arrived in the Niarelà quarter at the Dakan

Hotel. My companion had turned on his flashlight to figure out where we were; I saw only shadows in the garden of a detached house built in colonial style. I heard confabulations in the dark. Moussa and his squire, a boy of nine, talked to the hotel's attendant in the dark. Only later did I understand the goings-on, partly because at that moment I wasn't considering the four Frenchmen who were also on the minibus as our rivals. Stepping down from the bus, I even said good-bye with a funny little quip in their own language, but later I found them again in the shadows in front of a bungalow savagely fighting with the night attendant and Moussa in order to get into the rooms they had reserved. They must have been the best rooms, and Moussa was trying to screw the French so that we could get them, while the one we ended up in was the worst of the worst. Mosquitoes entered in swarms through the air conditioner, inoperable but with large openings inside thrown into the bargain, as if they had intentionally chipped away at it with a pick. Then in the dark Moussa wanted to know what time we wanted to get up, and Jean said, "Noon." That way, the next morning at ten, we thought, we would be free of him and we could be on our way. As soon as we woke up, there he was, waiting for us along with his squire; they had slept in the garden on the swing, miserable from mosquito bites, but they had guarded us the entire night.

6   At the root of our capture is my ineptness, which had pulled us under the sway of Moussa's gang. I am always too easily captured, Jean brings it to my attention. He says I look too much like I'm out for a stroll and that the locals smell a *pingone* waiting to be milked. To make up for my errors, I had suggested that we move to the Hôtel de l'Amitié, hurriedly pulled out of the tourist guide. We wanted to flee from the Hôtel Dakan, so full of mosquitoes, to find the air conditioning that would save us from malaria, to evade the fringe quarter Niarelà where Moussa had kept watch over us all night. But I will not forget my contentment at finding myself in the Niarelà quarter in the morning, with the red soil under my feet, the children who were there

looking at us, the women in doorways wearing colorful cloths wrapped around as skirts, the sky very luminous. In the morning the sky is whitish, but the light hits at such an angle that it has a glorious effect on colors. Nor will I forget how, when we requested a taxi, Moussa made a car appear instantly from around the corner by using some conjuring trick. It matters little if the marvel had been arranged by his little squire and that the car was a heap of metal sheets with handles that fell off in your hand, damp seats that got stuck to your pants, a hood held in place with a rope. The morning apparition in the Niarelà quarter must be one of the local miracles.

7 A foggy evening on the Niger. It is not the rainy season, but the season of desert winds. Soon Ramadan will begin, and Lent. It isn't fog that makes the view so opaque, but sand suspended in air that makes the sky look almost white during the day, even though the sand is red. On the hotel balcony it's almost an inch thick, incredibly fine sand, dust suspended in air, and with the heat of the sunlight, it gives everything the air of an astigmatic vision. It's because of the sand on the streets all around here, red soil at the edges of the asphalt, or else red soil with no asphalt, in the more peripheral neighborhoods. Behind the hotel's pool are trees, and this is the only place with trees in the entire city, to protect the tourists who go swimming or play golf on the enormous course along the bank of the Niger. Car headlights move very slowly across the long, narrow bridge that crosses the Niger, while the television transmits news about the massacres in Rwanda, the failed civilization in black Africa, leaving one to understand that in Europe, by contrast, everyone lives calmly and peacefully. All the repertory needed to make one feel a civilized spectator protected behind glass.

8 We have become friends with Ibrahim Traoré, a skinny boy-driver who stations himself in the hotel bar looking for customers. He comes from a Malinka village, son of a Malinka man and a Tuareg woman. His father was in the military at the time of the clashes with the Tuareg north of Gao, and when he was up there, he married a local woman. Ibrahim has something of the Tuareg in his features and in his very dignified bearing, always calm and collected in his gestures, precise with every word. He tells many stories about his father who comes from a village on the Guinea border, explaining that his language is Malinka, which is distinguished from the Bambara language by certain words and idioms. The last time his father returned from his village, he took him aside and told him he had to get married because he had found a wife for him in the village. Next year, the wedding will be down there. In the darkness of the bar, Ibrahim, looking like a boy who is calm and diligent, smilingly explains to us that he will marry without ever having seen his bride-to-be. His father has decided this, he can do nothing about it, although it does not seem to me that the thing bothers him very much. The choice of a wife from so far away is the result of this: since his family origins are in the village on the Guinea border, should problems arise with his new wife, he will be able to turn to the elders to state his complaints. If, instead, he married a girl from Bamako, to whom could he turn? If he's not happy with her, he would have no one he could appeal to and that would result in divorce. Everything is resolved within the family, and the idea of independent social relationships seems as vague as karate films, which are very much in vogue here.

9 I'm always wanting to slip out into the streets of Bamako. Everywhere people are selling things and chatting with an admirable indolence. But no one has an air about them of drifting and not knowing what to do with themselves. Everything in the street moves in discontinuous fluxes, trailing-off busyness, frequent encounters, continual deviations off the path. Movements that are busy, yet meandering, in the space that is packed with human bodies and lively colors, and merchandise heaped into piles. Nothing gives the impression of being isolated, everything is wrapped up in the same clouds of dust and odors. In this continual rubbing up against people who speak as soon as they see you, without barriers that protect against approaches, I am forgetting the funereal privacy with which I live in England . . . Dream in which I realize that the faces seen while I'm walking around in Bamako are all the faces of people in their thirties or forties, at the most in their sixties like me. Even the behavior of the people is a thing from other times, always very composed, from the elderly to the babies, even when they assault you in order to sell you something.

10 In the life of a tourist who travels a bit far, I think that at a certain point, a question necessarily arises: "But what have I come here for?" A question that sets in motion the great cinema of justification to oneself, so that one doesn't have to seriously say to oneself: "I'm here to do nothing." Boys like Moussa and Mohammed are well aware of this fact: they have to capture their tourist in order to help him in the job of doing nothing from morning till night. Because in all places in the world, men always have something to do, and this is the greatest marvel in the world, the harmony of habits that no one has decided upon, the confused beauty of the animatedness of cities. A tourist, instead, is a phantom who hangs around, dazed, outside of that single harmonious dream, precisely because he has been transported to a place to not do anything, except spend money. In Bamako's bustle, everyone has something to do, but if I understand it correctly, what one has to do is to sell something every day, to do something without thinking about it, to chat tranquilly in the cloud of dust, then go back home in the evening. Elementary functioning of business, daily life of sustenance, where I still ask myself, what is the profit? What is the profit of the cigarette vendor in front of the hotel who sells perhaps ten packs a day? And the profit of the woman selling ten bananas total, on a little table in the street?

11 This morning a car ride with Ibrahim. When we exited the hotel, it was as if he had grown in stature, everyone looked at him with interest and respect because he had work. It was an exit so triumphant that the gang of boys did not dare go near him. Ibrahim drives with an air of complete composure in the midst of traffic that would make a Neapolitan cab driver go insane. The Grand Marché, the Grand Poste: cars and bicycles all in a snarl, you cannot get through. On the sidewalk, piles of flowered material, broad damasks, skirt-cloths in brilliant color, the white boubous exposed to the red sand, the indigo covers with tribal designs. Signs on the street: AFRIQUE AUTO, Pièces Détachées (Spare Parts), DIRECTION NATIONALE DES AFFAIRES ECONOMIQUES, DIRECTION NA-TIONALE DE LA GEOLOGIE DES MINES, LA MAISON DE L'ARTISANAT, LUX BEAUTÉ, Boubakar Keita . . . A line of poles of leather slippers, golden *babouches,* sandals made of rubber. Cans containing every possible kind of canned food. A host of oil lamps. An armada of incredibly colored basins. The great mosque. A boy with his backbone bent at an acute angle and his head almost on the ground, a crippled angel who moves tranquilly through the crowd. Great big sacks of flour every twenty meters. A troupe of children who are running off. Paper and rags flying above the asphalt . . . We stop to get gas at a station that still has the old sign of the pony of the Cortemag-giore Company. Up ahead, leaning against a wall, a Tuareg with Ray-Ban sunglasses, a Sarankolé with a blue turban, another straight ahead who is maybe a Peul. I inquire, I would like to be able to recognize the different populations. A crippled old man approaches to sing us a song, but he leaves right away. Ibrahim says he comes from Gao ("a neighbor of the Tuareg"). There are three mango trees in front of the gas station, and a guy is lean-ing against a tree cleaning his teeth with a little stick that serves as toothpaste. Here in the morning everyone cleans their teeth with that same kind of little stick, and they seem content to be doing it, so it pleases me too.

12 Every morning I transcribe my notes, and I find names of places, lists of various things seen on the street, faces, clothing, bicycles, turbans, slippers, posters, little barber shops, children trying to snag a tourist, etc. The whole cloud of nothing in particular that wraps around us each day, inside and outside the hotel, indescribable. Then there is the good company of Ibrahim, who speaks with pleasure in the style of legends, and tells us about his grandfather, magical hunter, who went into the forest alone and with a single cartridge killed many beasts. (I have heard this story in our parts as well, except there it was the bragging of drunks.) Ibrahim says that with his magic arts he could go outside his body to meet people one hundred kilometers away, to find out news from distant, distant villages. It seems that in the village even his cousin had the ability to leave his body and take the form of savanna beasts, hyena, snake, bird. Him, however, he hasn't seen him in a long time.

13 That there no longer exists a colonial regime is perhaps an abstraction like many others, which at any rate counts for little in what goes on between white visitors and the black population. The concentration camp for tourists where we are does a good job of carrying out its function as a colonial entrenchment in the midst of the black population, with air conditioning that drives away the mosquitoes and doormen that drive away the unbridled assaults on the whites. The only thing allowed in the hotel is the presence of licensed indigenous sellers, with exhibits of statuettes in strategic points and their persecution of guests at every hour of the day. The white man is offered up to the internal market as one who automatically purchases tribal statuettes, just like he automatically gulps down colossal breakfasts in the morning. Then, if he wants, there are also the lovely prostitutes in the bar as well, admitted perhaps by the staff at the reception desk, which resembles a ministry staff a bit. From the signs in front of the various administrative offices, in colonial French, one understands that the state is now wearing the pants of the colonial administration, just so it can screw the lid of its abstractions on these people who live and conduct business just as they have always done. (Heavy discussions. I'm finding nothing else to write about, but it's because of the overcast sky and the closeness.)

14 Today I was talking with Jean about the fact that in Europe the passion of business seems like a means to an end, and the end is only profit, which permits you to do something you want behind the walls of your privacy. Here, instead, it seems that living and doing business are the same thing, the same stuff as the hours of the day, for which the goal of profit is not separated from the chatting and the cloud of dust, and rarely are the encounters reduced to an anonymous rendering of services, except to adapt itself to the customs of the white cow. For example, yesterday Ibrahim instructed me on how to buy pants; it is permitted to tell lies, such as finding a nonexistent defect in the pants; however, it is important to negotiate very delicately in order to reach a kind of amicable agreement, as if among relatives *(comme en famille)*. Then the encounter with the young businessmen behind the cathedral: the stalls filled with pants hanging from the ceiling, voices and confusion in the small sunny street, a handcart full of stones pulled by children, a beggar with a gnawed-away nose who came inside to beg me for alms. The desire to haggle disappeared. The radio was transmitting a beautiful dirge, which had the same turn of notes as in an American blues song.

15 Jean is supposed to meet the director of the Mali Center for Cinematography, a famous enough director whom one can never find. In the meantime, he telephones in search of Thomas Harlan, who is probably in America trying to convince the Americans about his daring project. This project consists of a series of films and documentaries made traveling all over the world with an itinerant company of actors, cineasts, cameramen, puppeteers, students. Jean's documentary should be part of it, if everything goes well. At dinner with Aïssata Diallò (a friend of a friend of Jean who studied in Paris), the talk was about this documentary on traveling to Bandiagara and on the Dogon healers at the Center for Traditional Medicine. It seems to me that when Jean talks about it no one ever understands what it is he wants to do, but when he pronounces the magic word "project," everyone seems to understand it perfectly.

16 Evening meditations after the assaults of the boys on the Avenue Keita, where that Mohammed with the maimed arm reappeared, a little offended even because I no longer have a desire to be at the mercy of his eloquence. We white tourists are like cows to be milked due to a sense of natural justice, and the whole game of milking the tourist resembles that of a colony of parasites that attach themselves to some large blood-filled animal. But I also have the idea that we would be only wan phantoms if the little black boys did not conjure us up for some brief moment in the animation of their world. I look on the street at tourists like me: they have the same uniform, money belts for documents around their waists, clothing that is somewhere between sportswear and beachwear, legs naked like children on vacation, technical equipment, sun hats. But above all, they have this in common: they avoid looking at one another, almost as if they are ashamed of recognizing each other. Each of us moves inside two cubic meters of an empty driven space, destined to look at everything as if from behind a window. Each one is inside the walls of his own privacy which he has carried along with him from home, he has reached his goal, but perhaps he has already lost everything along the way. I had these thoughts upon seeing a model British family, father, mother, son, daughter, in the big department store Somiex.

17 I took a ride as far as the entrance to the road to Sogoniko. Heavy traffic completely immersed in the cloud of red sand. They were also doing road repairs, everything in confusion, potholes, barricades. The natural disorder of life. Peugeot vans from the fifties were laden with people clinging to them everywhere. Bicycles, even some stacked with heavy stuff, with skinny riders who struggled in the midst of the beastly traffic.

Small carts pulled by donkeys, broken-down cars everywhere, small military vans. Hotels, embassies, car repair shops, beauty salons, stores with all types of European merchandise represented, signs for Marlboro. Ramshackle little detached houses, overrun with bougainvillea, and on the top the concave satellite dish. In a dirt clearing at the side of the street, planted alone in the vague terrain, was a puppeteer with a jangling marionette that was almost a meter tall. This marionette, long nose, chin jutting out, dressed like a European, was in clothes that were too tight (but made completely out of wood); he seemed to me the same as our own Totò. He even made the same gestures with his arms. From what ancient country does Totò's mask come? Where does his comicality originate, containing within it all of life's disorder that is found in these places? I would have liked to approach him, to chat with the puppeteer, but in this horrid traffic it was impossible to stop, let alone consider crossing the street. As in a dream, I talk about it with Jean: let Totò be our patron saint on this journey.

18 In a hurry to leave Bamako and to leave this hotel of Amity, where we're wasting money just to take shelter in air conditioning. Moreover, another siege seems imminent, given that one of the prostitutes stationed at the bar has targeted Jean. This one is dressed up in supreme elegance, like a princess from the times of the emperor Kankan Moussa. The fact is that as soon as she sees Jean, the black princess follows him into the elevator speaking sweet little words to him ("I'll lay you in your room, my little one"), and, what's more, when he runs to barricade himself in the room, she whispers to him through the door ("Open up for me, my little one"), such that he has to put wax plugs into his ears so as not to hear her, and he wakes me up at night saying that she's still on the other side of the door.

19 A strong desire to go back to the Niarelà quarter where we landed the first night. Perhaps inspired by the dinner with the beautiful Aïssata Diallò, who cannot understand how that quarter can possibly attract me so much. Ibrahim takes us there by car and winds through sandy streets where I see women with buckets and cans at a water pump. Many small shops with wooden doors covered with business nameplates, like when I was a child. Maybe that's why I am attracted to this quarter, it reminds me of something. For example, the shop of the bicycle and auto mechanic. But I don't remember what it reminds me of . . . Streets of red soil, full of potholes, crossing at right angles. Three left crippled by leukemia, a lot of graffiti on the courtyard walls. A woman crouched down in the sand sells oranges. A man sawing an iron rod in the middle of the street. Multicolored clothes hung out to dry in a courtyard. A little boy tiredly dragging a bucket of water. Here, a huge poster: CELLULE D'APPUI POUR L'INSERTION DES JEUNES PILOTS. Who knows what this means? In front of decaying little houses built in the French style, two very thin cows are wandering about on their own. It makes me wonder whether they are sacred cows. Jean: "We're not in India, you know." Oh, right, right! . . . Just outside the Niarelà quarter, a tremendous nondescript cement building with an enormous sign: NIGHT CLUB METRO-POLE. Countryside, the first hazy terrain, a lot of truck and bicycle traffic. I already see the savanna in the distance, in the red sandy dust clouds that engulf cars and trucks. "Savanna" is the word that makes me imagine most *la brousse,* the bush. That is why I'm in a hurry to leave.

20 Going toward Ibrahim's house, you see districts that seem ravaged by war, if for no other reason than the asphalt is one big pothole. Maybe not even asphalt, but more like a chalky pavement that crumbles into pieces. Opening on the horizon in the direction of a quarter called Niarere Courò. We pass in front of a gas station that consists of little tables with five or six bottles of gasoline set on top. Or else, some that are transparent tubes that contain a few liters of oily stuff, a handle to pump gas, and that's it. Approaching the Niger, it seemed to me like being in the countryside, even if there are many trucks kicking up whirlwinds of dust, and then there on a low rise two young women who beat cereal, *fonio*, inside mortars with long poles. I ask myself why they went to beat the grain right there at that particular place, among the clouds of red sand, to prepare dinner for their husbands. Beautiful young women, they have an arch in their backs that comes in a great deal above the kidneys, so that the so-called seat sticks out like a curl. Before having seen the Niger from a distance, I made note of the women who were selling lemons (they look like lemons but they're oranges), their austere beauty. The Niger is full of islets, a steep red bank, farther down we see life along the river. The broad colorful cloths hung out to dry, people making bricks and drying them in molds. Men repairing nets, women washing clothes. Here I see nude men washing themselves in one inlet, in another inlet the women are washing themselves, and they have separate little corners for bathing in the river. Ibrahim too comes to bathe here, he says, on Saturdays.

21 Yesterday, passing over a little bridge that was falling to pieces, Ibrahim told us that a hyena was seen in this area, but he thinks it was not a hyena but rather someone who transformed himself into a hyena at night. These are his preferred subjects. He confirmed for me all the warehouses full of hearsay about African magic that I have stored up in my head. ("C'est ça; voilà!") Then he gave me an overview of the magic healers in his quarter. I saw in passing many white cubical houses, prefabricated maybe on top of a foundation of reinforced cement. In the preceding quarter, on the other hand, there were traditional houses made of *banko*, that is to say, clay and straw, little villages with goats and chickens wandering about. Ibrahim's house is one of those big white boxes that appear to be prefabricated, planted on an empty street. Beneath a balcony, four little girls played a game with pieces inside a box. They were Ibrahim's sisters and they offered us tea, continuing to play. But since we had replied with a conventional no, they paid no more attention to us afterwards. Ibrahim wanted us to meet his father, who, however, wasn't there. As for the old lady introduced as mother, seated in the house behind a raffia blind, I had doubts as to how to place her because Ibrahim said that his father has two wives. I could not place the atmosphere, because it was in a quarter on the outskirts of the city, but you breathed the air of the savanna. (The pace of life perhaps does not change much, whether here or in the village. The villages of the quarter make group decisions, the way the elders of the village do, everything controlled by the family.) Near Ibrahim's house, there is a healer who cures cervical illnesses by killing a chicken, but right next to him is the sign for a SALON DE BEAUTÉ, and a little farther on writing on a wall, ROBERTO BAGGIO, together with goats and sheep grazing at the side of the road. Behind the house, a trash heap, and there four young black men, robust, with closely cropped hair, were resting on a step. Ibrahim introduced them as his big brothers and they cheerfully treated him like a puppy. ("He's a good boy.") They talked about inviting us to dinner one night, but we left shortly thereafter.

22 Everything we were supposed to do in Bamako has gone poorly. Always enchanted and lost in thought, we waited too long to go to the bank. Now Ramadan has begun and the banks don't open until Monday, and for this reason, tomorrow we will have to leave with French francs and a very few CFA that some guy on the street got for us at a better exchange rate than at the hotel. The director of the Mali Center for Cinematography, with whom Jean was supposed to meet, is making a film in Mauritania. We've got vague information about the place where we're supposed to be staying in Bandiagara. A caretaker at the Center for Traditional Medicine said by phone that everything was ready for two people who were due to arrive: but are we those two people? Understanding names on the telephone in these places is not very easy.

23 Jean under siege by the black princess. As soon as she sends whispered messages through the door ("It's me, my little one") he runs to hide under the covers with his wax ear plugs so as not to hear that sorceress voice. So then it's me who must take the situation in hand, you understand. It's me who is the responsible man, who goes out to confront the siren. Being both old and a little deaf as well, I'm immune to every seduction. But she is more clever than I am, and every time, she vanishes from the hall into thin air, leaving me feeling let down. Strange, however, that we don't see the black princess strolling in the bar's shadows anymore, but she reappears with her beguiling voice only when we are in bed. Yesterday evening I inspected the bar prostitutes, she was not there. An hour later, we heard her voice from behind the door, I leaped from bed to confront her, and she had vanished from the hall, leaving, however, the trace of her perfume. Does she think she can seduce me with the trick of perfume? Tall, almost taller than me, dressed from the times of the emperor Kankan Moussa, she might just succeed. As a bewitched white man, I must be very careful.

24 Moussa strikes again. This evening, an ambush in front of the hotel by his gang, however, with a different head, less arrogant and more determined than Mohammed. This one gave us a real interrogation, after having us militarily surrounded by his little boys. Given that we were going to Dogon country, he suggested a Land Rover and told us we had to agree to a contract. It ended up that Jean, irritated, made his escape, and I reverentially ceded our arms: "Tomorrow?" "At what time?" "Noon." "No, at ten." Impossible to dispute with these people because in discussions I always take a beating. Tomorrow we've got to slip out before ten to the station where the bus leaves for Sogoniko in order to catch a bus and liberate ourselves from this gang, never mind the siren behind the door . . . At the dinner hour, in front of the hotel some Italians were pulling, with some force, on a guy the color of *caffé latte,* who was wearing an oversized white shirt, his turban askew. The guy was recalcitrant, and then the two who were dragging him by the arm got tired and told him to fuck off. The woman who was with them, on the other hand, had not given up yet, and, tugging him by the sleeve, said to him in Italian, "Come on, come to dinner, silly." Tiny, in sportswear, she put on a show of rude gestures, the likes of which I have never seen here, where everyone is so composed. Who knows why they wanted so badly to drag him along? Contrary to us, who were running away from Moussa's gang, these people maybe needed filler in their little touristic evening out.

SECOND NOTEBOOK

1 Eleven o'clock. We're traveling in a bus that is falling apart at the seams, the only whites among black passengers packed in like sardines. The open question is where we will sleep in Bandiagara and whether we are the two whom they're expecting. Problem of being low on cash because of the banks being closed in Bamako. They told us that credit cards are useless up north. On the first row of the bus, there are four soldiers, armed, heads shaved, sleeping. Next to us, a man with hazelnut skin, an intellectual manner, uniform of a functionary, he is reading *Les Echos,* the newspaper of the movement that overthrew the pro-Soviet government. At the stop for prayers in open countryside, it is he who is the first to spread out his prayer rug and bow to God . . . The sun bakes your head, there's only a straw canopy under which to take shelter, but the stones for sitting in the shade are already taken. Now all the kneeling passengers are praying, except for the soldiers and the two of us. A swarm of children arrive from the savanna with little sacks of madeleines, bananas and grapes, green tangerines, plastic containers filled with yogurt. An assault that interrupts the praying of many. A soldier, face of an Algerian, with a suspicious expression, observes me writing, as he drinks his little yellow container of yogurt.

2 Along the street, very colorful governmental posters. In one, drawings of six black youths dressed like Europeans (except for one in indigenous clothing). They seem a little confused on a foreshortened street that represents the prospects for the future. Underneath, the anti-AIDS propaganda has three big nouns: Prudence, Family, Condoms. (In Mali, AIDS is more widespread than in other African countries; however, many here say that it has always existed and that it comes from the Ivory Coast.) Another poster shows the same foreshortening, but in this view of the future, there is a girl who goes to school, dressed like a European college student. The words of the educational campaign say that this girl will become a producer for the economy and a producer of offspring for the state. In my wanderings, I have not seen anyone who resembles the figures in the state posters, who seem to me like birds in an aviary, while those of us in transit on a bus are more like migratory birds.

3 On arrival in Ségou, I get very irritated with Jean, who bolted out of the bus station in search of a taxi and hired the first one he found without bargaining over the price. It's me who is in charge of the finances, it's me who is the responsible man! A taxi more broken-down than this one has never existed, with a driver who does not speak French and even seems to be a little dim. On the contrary, he was not the least bit dim, because the ride from the bus station to the hotel was no more than seven hundred meters, but he asked for a figure which was enough to go halfway across Bamako. Nothing here is under control, money disappears like water. I realize I am becoming stingy.

4 Ségou, morning. During the night, my avarice became more marked. I even had a dream in which I was Molière's miser. I'm always keeping track of what we're spending, of how much is left to get to Bandiagara. I shudder at the thought of being without money in this unfamiliar town where they don't accept credit cards. As soon as we arrive in Bandiagara, I should have my head cured by the Dogon healers, and while I'm at it they can cure my ears as well . . . We're having breakfast on the terrace of a restaurant called L'Auberge, which is run by a Lebanese man who yesterday evening presented us his credentials. All around, streets of red sand, dazzling light. Little children lie in wait for us at the exit. A woman passes by with a basket of linens a meter high on her head, and she greets us. "Ça va?" "Oui, et vous, ça va?" "Un peu." (Are things okay? Yes, and you, things okay? Not bad.) Rare that they don't say hello here, because commerce and greeting go hand in hand. But I, from behind the protection that isolates the tourist from the rest of the world, greet whomever, just out of an idiotic sense of public spirit. In the meantime, the children wait for us to sell us something, making gestures, calling out to us again from the distance, after they have been chased away from the L'Auberge restaurant.

5 Jean doesn't want to do anything and perhaps this is because he is still under the spell of the sweet little voice of the princess behind the door. The only initiative he took was to carry the dirty laundry to a laundromat in front of our hotel. Yesterday evening we passed by the door of a tailor, and he went in to ask if he could make him a pair of pants before the end of today, an ill-advised question. The old Bambara tailor was done working for the day, he was in the process of putting on his beautiful azure boubou, he did not understand half a word of French. Unfortunately, Jean listened to my advice about the documentary he wants to make, which does not sit well, given the status of the serious-minded project. I do not like the idea of filming the Dogon healers while they're performing their healing rites, and even granting that they allow him to film them, it would be a folkloristic discount sale of magical secrets. So then I began to daydream about the alternatives, but an idea so baroque popped into my head that even my brain was confused.

6 Jean is looking for a fax machine to send Thomas Harlan messages, but the only fax machine he heard about, located in a fortified hotel with international flags along the river, didn't work. Streets intersect in a chessboard pattern, houses made of bricks laid without mortar, sand everywhere on the ground. In our ramblings we wander around with another gang of children who do not let go of us, plus the dogs and chickens that follow behind. In particular, there is a little boy who comes up to my navel, glued to my side, by the name of Gaous Dembelé, who keeps suggesting that he would be the ideal tourist guide for us. Another little boy baptized Hammadi insists upon selling us a Tuareg dagger, paying no attention to our refusals. Hammadi seems a little out of it to me, or else asleep in his commercial dreams, while the tiny Gaous is in a hurry to write down the address of his business in my notebook, with two telephone numbers.

7 Seated, watching life along the Niger. On the horizon, a village of straw huts where the weavers of local rugs live. Long pirogues, ten meters long, arrive. Bare-breasted women hang laundry on the beach. Nudity in public is banned, no one walks around with short pants except children. The Europeans in shorts naturally are thought of as overgrown children—for example, this morning the American with her legs exposed as if she were on campus. On the river, though, nudity of the breasts is frequent, from girls to mature women who have already nursed many children. They enter the water to bathe themselves with a rag around their hips, without the look of someone worried about being watched. While we are voyeurs who would like to make the world nude and spy on it through a keyhole, this much is certain.

8 Later, 3 p.m. Pirogues arriving in the Niger, in one is a Tuareg or a Peul, helped ashore at the dock. On the beach, an expanse of beautiful, colorful clothing, elsewhere an expanse of bricks laid out to dry. Hard work getting a cow off the pirogue, it has huge horns like those of the Maremma, entirely black with mottled spots of decoration around its neck. Now the disembarking cow absolutely refuses to stand up, while the sheep carried to be washed in the river raised up their voices in bleats like a Greek chorus. The incredibly fat ram tied to a boat nervously

\text{}

watches the event, then while they push more sheep into the water, he lowers his head and butts it into two men. In the water, they wash clothes, men and women soap themselves, matrons with very colorful basins rinse the wash, a gentleman with a turban looks like he's meditating, nude children are thrashing in the water. Everything all mixed together among boats and sheep and laundry and pirogues, but everything is ceremonial, an order within the disorder. The angle of the sun regulates the cadence of every move, like tropisms according to the hour of sunlight. I would like to follow every moment taking notes, to write down all that I can, but rhythm is worth more than concepts for capturing the world.

9 Negotiations at sunset with children who want to sell us something. You say no, they come forward as if you've said nothing. However, they do not want to talk about money. On the subject of price, they always say generic things: "How much?" "It's not expensive." "But how much?" "Whatever you want." You repeat that you don't want to hear any more about it, but they do not take this as a termination of the negotiations, merely a pause in the transaction, saying again the next moment: "Tomorrow then?" "No." "Okay, whenever you want." Always coming back to the renewal of negotiations, calm and dignified. At eight or ten years of age they have already suckled in the spiritual essence of Islamic commerce, which is above all the adventure of contact among people.

10 In front of the hotel: display of statuettes and rugs, with vendors spread out in the sand. On the corner, an open-air cinema, a naked wall that seems like one from a prison, with two holes blackened by smoke: ticket window number one, ticket window number two. A karate film is being projected onto the wall, and the children want to take us there to see it, alluding to the fact that they don't have money to enter. Later, in the dark, a deaf-mute boy using gestures insisted on taking us to a *tam tam*, where one dances. He started to dance in the middle of the street, making savage guttural sounds. At this point, I had to summon up all my mimetic talents to explain that we were tired. Then the other one started in again about the karate film, asking me for money with very elaborate gestures. In the end, I wanted him to touch my pockets to see for himself that I had no money with me, and this convinced him to leave me alone. Physical contact with whites is avoided. Naturally, he too left with a wave, talking about future negotiations. His hand turning in a spiral, as if to say: "We'll see each other later, tomorrow, etc., you'll pay, you'll pay, Inshallah!"

11 In the night, a bird cries: "Qwouak qwouak." Little Gaous has explained: "It is the *ghinghi,* which eats the heart." A bird that eats the hearts of men, the muezzin who continues to call Allah, and we profane tourists feel amazement behind our protective glass. Little carts with huge stones pass by pulled by skinny little asses; a carter gave me a military salute: "At your command, captain" . . . Ségou is a small city that can be crossed on foot in two hours. Old capital of the Bambara reign, occupied during the last century by Toucouleur conquerors who built the still-existing Koranic schools, then at the end of the 1900s the victorious French made it into an agricultural center. This is a place I would happily stay. There are five high schools, they say. Place suitable for writing, I could stop here, if only they accepted credit cards. I would spend my time watching life on the Niger, maybe I would put on a tie for strolling in the evenings on the streets of sand, along with the chickens who wander around in freedom.

12 A lizard six inches long is wiggling around at my feet. So many jeeps in the hotel's courtyard that it looks like a post office. They are the cars of people who are driving the Paris-Dakar road rally. The L'Auberge has all its walls papered all over with decals exalting the virtues of the Paris-Dakar. Yesterday, on television, they were interviewing the race drivers, but mostly they showed vehicles that were covered with sand or had overturned in the desert. Television capers down in the desert. Discussion at the bar between white travelers and the Lebanese owner, the usual sports talk, the famous names whose mere utterance produces an outburst of noise. I listened, exchanging sympathetic winks with the big black lady behind the bar, the strong and decisive type, whom the waiters instantaneously obey. I gave her a wink to say she was right, we understood each other: you just obey her and that's it. If I were to stay, I would have already found a source of support in this black matron, very substantial and efficient, I too would instantaneously obey her.

13 Morning on the Niger. About ten children watch me write, mute, from a distance, until the tiny Harouna creeps up on all fours to steal a look at the underside of my notebook to discover the secrets it holds. When I grab him by the ear, he justifies himself: "You American? I speak English." I don't interest him as a writer, but as a fake American, because here all Americans become a single undifferentiated American, who will do, even if fake. He is the ultimate of what you represent as a white . . . Jean still in search of a fax to send messages to Thomas Harlan, and of a telephone to call Bandiagara and find out about our lodging. One waits, time passes, and I'm not in any hurry to leave, plus we're not spending much money here. I've met the antiquarian of the place, an authentic Dogon gentleman, who sells very beautiful statues in a dark cave: Aboulaye Teme, with a gray caftan and a blue *cecìa*.

14 The big black lady has asked me if I take photographs. In a raptus of good feelings toward her, I confessed that I take photographs by writing. She lowered her head; I wanted to explain it to her. I had tripped myself up, and she didn't understand anything, then she didn't have time for the lucubrations of a writer on vacation. In moments like this, one catches a glimpse of what there could have been, of what fine impressions he could have made in life, if only he were not constrained to be what he is. For a moment, a happy brightness dazzles, exposed to the benevolent look of another human being, this is how fantasies are born and the journey becomes more varied. Then, naturally, you realize that you were born in another place, human goodwill has its limits, and words are clothes hung out to dry in the wind that easily lose their color.

15 We leave without being able to understand what awaits us in Bandiagara. We shall see. At the bus station in Ségou, waiting for a bus that is an hour late, there is a young Frenchman with an enormous backpack on the bench, as well as a plump gentleman from Kayes, Mali, who lives in France. Conversation with the plump man, who hands me his social security card as if it were a calling card. I duly copy it into my notebook, he seems satisfied to me . . . I forgot to tell about the encounter yesterday with a lady who was on the plane with us, a scientist of Italian origin who is part of an international committee on the prevention of malaria. When she learned we were going to Mopti, she got us worried, saying that in Mopti there is a mosquito with an absolutely incurable bite, and that we needed to run immediately to the pharmacy and get vaccinations. Now, Jean has gone off to the pharmacy to get information. A boy arrives on a motorbike, with a shaved head, dark mobster sunglasses, admired by his companions, overgrown kids who are milling around the ticket office. The gentleman from Kayes in the meantime has begun praying in an enclosure of sand, kneeling on a towel. Jean comes back: the pharmacist said that she is from Mopti and the idea about the assassin-mosquito is just a legend.

16 The bus has stopped along the main road to Mopti, in front of a kind of shop or a country bar. Everyone gets off, many go to pray, you don't know how long this stop is going to last. Inside there is a large room with plank beds, the seated men watch the karate championship on television. Extremely loud noise. From the courtyard comes a female Bambara voice singing, very shrill, the shrillness is part of the timbric invention. I go and sit down on the steps, the tea vendor hands me a small glass. Children clustered around my feet. (The old colonial model of khaki canvas attracts them even more than Jean's modern desert boots.) Food stands in front of the shop, but the vendors sleep peacefully on the ground in the middle of the comings and goings. It is Ramadan, people eat only at night. Life is lived close to the ground, with low voices, without trills, even among the women. A perpetual disorder, swarming, but without tension. People look around a great deal, chat a great deal, then when they are tired, they lie down on the ground to sleep. A youth in complete Adidas uniform kindly offers Jean a carrot . . . Only broken-down cars pull up in front of this shop. The new thing does not exist here, everything is worn out and used, as if they were consuming the discards of European beasts. In our countries of gaudy wealth these people are considered to be miserable. But the man with the tattered jacket, the skeletal toothless woman, the children with rags on their backs, that man who is sleeping under a table, seem to me to be without anxiety and without complaint. Strange that for us, complaint is the rule in nearly all the well-off people I know, almost an automatic cock-a-doodle-doo of the self.

17 In front of that store, Jean gave me an orange and then I didn't know where to throw away the peels. I looked for a trash can, while the ground was a carpet of garbage, trash paper, mud, peelings, rotten food and cans. But I was looking for an official place to dispose of my trash still, out of some idiotic sense of civic-mindedness. A little girl motioned to me that I could throw the peels on the ground, then she laughed with delight upon getting a better look at me, as if I were a charming fool. Jean says that I have been infected with the manias of the English. Exactly! I have become ecologic and biodegradable, I make even the chickens laugh here. Among other things, I have lost a sense of time, I don't know what day it is today.

18 Finally, I can really see the savanna, but I still don't understand a thing about it. For a while, scattered villages have unfolded, circular villages of mud huts, with roofs made of bundles of sheaves. The granaries begin to resemble those of the Dogon, pyramidal in shape, with an empty space at the base to prevent mice from climbing up. They are situated in the center of the enclosure of the village. A series of termites' nests along the street, and I understand why they have been compared to palaces, they are fantastic architectural works. Some of them are a meter and a half high, constructions similar to large mushrooms . . . Around six o'clock, the sun is no longer dazzlingly bright, white streaks everywhere. A lone woman out on the savanna, with a large package on her head; she walks slowly as if she were out for a stroll. Jean notes that for two hours an absolute calm has reigned on the bus, no one talks, no one smokes. On the buses in India, on the other hand, everyone talks and smokes, Jean says, and you're all jammed in together like here. Sky almost entirely white, flat land to infinity. With stripped limbs, the baobabs sway, spectral contortions of a famished spirit of the savanna. Other villages where you see that it's already evening because the solar tropisms have become less intense. Calmness without any waiting for the world to be different from that which it is, so therefore something goes well.

19 Stop at San. The detached houses in French colonial style that I saw passing brought to mind a thousand and one nights . . . There is a road here that forks off to Djenné. For an entire lifetime, a desire to go to Timbuktu; now I know that Timbuktu is only a poor copy of Djenné, a couple of hours from here. Djenné is the city of the magnificent houses, Africa's most famous mosques, of roofs on the river where René Callié slept when he went on foot from Guinea, disguised as an Arab, the first white to see these marvels. However, stinginess prevents me from going to Djenné, because I'm still working out our finances. Jean would have said yes, but it's dark now, the bus for Djenné has left.

20 Still in San, as night falls. A young man from our bus, tall, likable, well-dressed, sits down beside me as I smoke a cigarette on a little wall. I offer him a cigarette, he explains that since yesterday, he's been *gâté*. In his way of speaking this means that he's got a problem. He lost his wallet with all his money and he's on his way to his sister's house in Sévaré to get help, otherwise he doesn't know how he's going to get himself out of the mess. He comes from Abidjan, he lives in Bamako and sells suits there like the one he's got on, modeled after the suit always worn by the president of Mali, a style with three pockets, which is why the president of Mali is called the Three-Pockets Man. Seeing as we too are getting off in Sévaré, he will guide us in the dark to the Hôtel Debo. I am happy to have made friends with him, and I try to convince Jean to buy himself a suit like the president's.

21 Long trip in the dark, hours and hours, with the half-moon shining, campfires next to the huts along the street, and the sense of navigating blindly through a deserted wilderness, which was reinforced when, after San, there were no more villages, only spectral baobabs in the headlights. Jean says he saw a hyena . . . Truly extraordinary, the calm on the bus. Many women with babies, some of whom are nursing, and you do not hear a baby cry for the entire trip. Jean tries to sleep, but it is a difficult undertaking due to the amazingly forceful shaking on asphalt that is full of potholes.

22 We arrive in this pit of the world, Sévaré, in the pitch-dark. We get off in front of a gas station, TOTAL, which shines in the dark. The attendants come out to shake our hands, they don't know where the hotel is. Neither was our tailor from Abidjan better oriented, headed toward his sister's in search of money to return to Bamako. In the dark, we talked about seeing each other again in Bamako and he said, "Inshallah." This word struck my secret Islamic chord, that is why I pulled out some money and gave it to him to get him out of his predicament.

More than a kilometer on foot in the thick darkness, with the heavy pack on my back. I was walking in front, and at a certain point I passed by a little light in a hut. There were some girls on the main road, I came up in the dark, and I asked them from behind if they knew where the hotel was. They ran off, terrified, howling, because they had taken me for a ghost or an evil spirit of the savanna. They were right, I too felt myself to be a phantom. Finally, landed in this hole called Hôtel Debo, on a lane made of sand, at the end of the night. As soon as we were in, Jean read me a passage from a travel book, which says this: often those from Abidjan introduce themselves as tailors and say that they have lost their wallet in order to sponge money off tourists. But that one wrote down his address in Bamako for me, in a beautiful handwriting, with strokes that were almost Arabic, the name of his father-in-law who works in the postal service, then three telephone numbers in a row.

23 Sévaré, Hôtel Debo. It could be a little pension for retirees on the Adriatic riviera, the same unadorned rooms, everything tiled in pseudo-modern style, same sad standard, with the difference that in the halls there are grasshoppers a finger and a half long, and all around there are villages of huts immersed in darkness. Long sleep to get strength back. Toward evening, in the restaurant, four men were watching the Milan-Vicenza soccer match on television, and they knew everything about the Italian soccer championship. They talked about it with Jean, who is an expert in this area as well and even has some pretty progressive notions about sports. Then they showed the Juventus-Atalanta match on the screen, the worst soccer one can see. Thai chicken, a mess-hall concoction that the Tuareg chef served me as if he were doing me a favor. I had to pretend to eat it because the so-called chef sat down next to me and kept an eye on me as he watched the vile soccer match.

24 In the dining room, a curly-haired young man began to talk to Jean, saying that he knows the Center for Traditional Medicine in Bandiagara, which is where we are supposed to go, very well. He knows Dr. Piero Coppo, who founded it, very well. He himself, with a truck, brought the bricks used to build the center. He knows the architect who planned it, an Italian who is now building something in Mopti. Perfect! He offered to take us to Bandiagara tomorrow in his truck, he didn't want to talk about money, appointment at ten. Mysterious and no-nonsense type, not particularly likable and modern. The soccer match finished, he walks over and says good-bye to us: "Tomorrow morning!" However, before we went up to bed, the owner of this little pension blocked our way on the stairs to have a discussion with us in a lowered voice so that no one would hear. He says that we are under the protection of the Hôtel Debo, and he must warn us. He has nothing against the curly-haired fellow who is supposed to take us to Bandiagara, but he would advise against going with him in the morning. There have been pirate-like attacks on tourists on the road to Bandiagara, where one is unprotected and anything can happen. There are check-points, but distant from each other, one can't rely on them. He doesn't want to accuse anyone, but it's better if tomorrow morning we go and find a bush taxi, get ourselves a contract, etc. This man has ruined for me the feeling of being in a place where one can trust others because everyone wants to do business with you and commerce is the lifeblood of friendship. Reminding me as well about that encounter at the bus station in Ségou, the plump gentleman-from-Kayes-but-living-in-Paris, a bit paternalistic toward his country ("they are not civilized"), who, when I asked him to watch my backpack, replied with noble words ("We are all brothers here.") However, he then left without saying good-bye, abandoning my backpack to the lizards, like a businessman who has no time to lose.

25 In the room, after the nighttime chat with Jean. There are certain mosquitoes here which fly around pronouncing a mysterious "Psst. Psst. Psst." I can't sleep because below us there is an electricity generator making a racket. Looking outside into

the dark, I see nothing except, far off, the lighthouse at the con-
fluence of the rivers, where Mopti is. All around crickets make
their monotonous calls, which at times I am unable to distinguish from the grasshopper buzzings in my ears. Every once in a
while, one can hear the bleating of a sheep, a cry of a distant bird.
Soon it will be dawn, and I haven't slept a wink. At a certain age,
sleep becomes light, one doesn't fall blissfully into the other
world, there is no longer the clear shifting between day and
night, but always a life in the border zone. Difficult sleep is a sign
of being closer to the dead, who in fact never sleep at all.

26 In Mopti, morning. Beautiful city, ancient, like the adventures of Ariosto and others. Discouraging negotiation at
the Hôtel Kananga, in order to have a credit card accepted in
exchange for some money. Come back! The manager can't . . .
According to Jean, coming over from Sévaré was indeed more
dangerous than making a parachute jump because of the driver's
driving style. I'll skip over trying to find the so-called bush taxi,
with a Tuareg on a bike who stayed right behind us so he could
sell us a Peul cap. A very beautiful cap which stinginess pre-
vented me from buying. Besides which, we definitely would have
been lost on the savanna with carrying heavy backpacks, run off
by soldiers because we had wound up in a sandy and militarized
zone, had the Tuareg on the bike not been persistent about selling us that Peul cap, amiably guiding us through narrow streets
of masses of run-down houses, as far as a little piazza that
looked like a dump for automobile carcasses. These were the so-
called *taxi de brousse,* bush taxis, and our driver was a skeletal
gentleman of very advanced age, who drove at maximum speed,
up and down the sandy rises in the road, in his completely
destroyed car, except for the exposed steering wheel column and
the essential controls. The door handles opened only with magic
moves from outside.

27 Hôtel Kananga, modern, airy, with a lovely garden, seems
like a lair of flesh-eating vultures who feed on human

bones. I argued with a boy driver who offered to take us to Bandiagara for the sum of 45,000 CFA, then reduced to 40,000, but immediately increased, saying we had to pay for the gas, which, according to another surly fellow affiliated with the Kananga, would bring it up 7,000 CFA. And while Jean was seen by the hotel manager, who refuses credit cards but will exchange French francs for a fee higher than the one paid in Bamako, I got on friendly terms with the boy driver who had caught up with me at the shore of the river to convince me that 40,000 CFA was an honest price. Then he boasted that his father has beautiful pirogues docked, plus many cars for tourists, etc. I went through the whole ridiculous routine for him, going through a whole litany of facts recited by a tourist-who-knows-the-ropes, who will not let himself be taken in by the locals. To which he promptly predicted our ruin, adding to that the lie that the bush taxis would not leave today, or tomorrow either, so that we will be trapped in Mopti forever.

28 In spite of Jean, who is tense and restless, I have an idiot's contentment to be here in Mopti. My mind is jumping around, it is making everything look like a marvel to me, or else like an evil, with many things known from before that flash into my head, being either a blessing or a curse, criticizing me with a harsh pedagogic voice while I stand on the brink of an abyss. Travel situations in places that disorient. You become an enchanted tourist without even wanting to be, always in search of a way to keep something under control. You have to find a little light at the height of your blackout, but it is, however, an indistinct twinkling; here or anywhere else, it makes no difference.

29 Hunkered down on a rock, I'm fine, if I write I don't think too much. I'm writing in the middle of the piazza where Mopti's market is. There's one passing by who looks exactly like Jesus Christ, much slimmed down however in the last few years. Another one on a bike who's weaving in and out between bales of cloth, and comes back among them to repeat a difficult turn.

No one is on a direct course, everyone meets someone and starts up again in a different direction, but this also has to do with the fact that it is impossible to go in a straight line in the midst of the massive quantity of stuff spread out in the piazza. Beverage vendors, immovable in the confusion. A man who's wearing an anti-smog mask arrives with his family, followed by his wife who has a heavy burden on her head, naked children who run behind her. Enormous trucks make enormous maneuvers among people who are lying on the ground. On the ground, sand, waste paper, peels from purchased bananas, flies, a confused-looking lizard. The tailor with his sewing machine, ensconced between a truck and a bus, repairs a piece of canvas and stops to chat with a friend. Two women with basins full of fish on their heads, the shoeshiner with his shoeshine box.

30 Two *toubabs* have arrived in the piazza—an indigenous word that translates exactly into the term "white *pingone*," invented by Jean. These two arriving in the piazza are tourists like us, but uptight Anglo-Saxon types, one being a little fat fellow, the other tall and thin, with big straw hats and equatorial garb. Jean comes back with a Coke, which he is chugging with excess force. We take note of the pride of the young woman who is guiding the two *toubabs*, who is dressed (the guide) in a flak jacket, as if for an adventurous journey on the frontier. What comes to mind is an Indian guide on the American frontier, a Natty Bumppo type, because here we're in the north and towards the border territory, where it is necessary to know the dialects and local tribes as Natty Bumppo did. Staying here, however, is a problem, because every ten seconds someone comes up wanting to sell me something.

31 Night in the courtyard of the Mauritanian Sidibouyé, who invited Jean yesterday evening. For a modest sum, we slept on the sand in his courtyard, even dined in his courtyard, served by young girls who were not Mauritanian in appearance, but who had very bejeweled ears. Nile perch, couscous with a peanut paste. Twilight chatting about Mopti, Djenné, the Mauritanian merchants who at one time controlled all commerce, the Tessalit caravan route, the one for the salt mines in Terhaza . . . The night began with a three-quarter moon. A short while ago up the street, I saw a dwarf with a drum, a dwarf like in our circuses. And I don't know why he plays the drum at night, almost hourly, behind the courtyard wall. Few bangs, but it was enough to keep me awake until very late. Someone unknown to us with a turban came to sleep in our courtyard when we were already in our sleeping bags, except he was lying on the ground under the canopy. Here everyone excels in sleeping, an enviable skill. I did not manage to close my eyes, every so often I would smoke a cigarette. Then I developed the idea that behind the wooden trellis with its openings there were two daughters of the Mauritanian who were spying on me and laughing at me. I had the idea that my defect of insomnia was making them laugh a great deal. I heard tittering, I kept my ears open. I turned over, with the sad inability to fall asleep exposed to the world like a dog or a cat. Finally, the muezzin.

32 Morning outing to banks in search of someone who will accept our credit cards. No one wants them . . . The children down there are playing foosball beneath the canopy of the Mopti kiosk. Toward the river, straw huts near a garbage dump, and outside their domed roofs, barbers display signboards with many newspaper clippings stuck onto them. These clippings show the various styles of "American cut"—haircuts like those of kids in the American ghetto, shaved off at the temples, with just a little crown at the top of the head, cuts with just a tuft right front, etc. A separate inquiry would be one on the styles of head coverings in circulation, which run from the dignified white skullcap to the red fezes, turbans of every color, woolen ski-mask caps (the heat notwithstanding), straw hats going up into cones, pith helmets, leather motorcyclists' caps, and, last, one who passes wearing a black hat like those worn by our village priests. You hear a woman singing on the radio, halfway between the

Portuguese *fado* and the muezzin's cry. On the back of the bus, Bob Marley passes by.

33 The two *toubabs* who yesterday appeared to me to be Anglo-Saxons, one short and chubby, the other tall and wiry, are in reality two Germans who have come by car from Europe. Having gone to sell the car in Togo, now they are going to the Dogon country and then by pirogue as far as Timbuktu. I was talking with the tall wiry one, who's maybe dyspeptic. Brutish German traveler who was in China for five years, sixty trips, three years in South America, thirty trips, and now he's doing all of Africa. Bitter, however, about the blacks, according to him only in Gambia is life good, because one senses the English education, while French-speaking blacks are aggressive and only want to rob you. We are waiting for the bush taxi to leave, but it's not leaving until it's jam-packed. A broken-down Peugeot 504 van, a model that hasn't been produced in more than thirty years. The luggage rack on the roof holds sacks of stuff that require two people to lift, plus all the travelers' baggage. Two extremely fat elderly people, two slender little girls, one dressed all in white like a *hajji* who will not answer me in any language. A woman with a beautiful face, a refined manner, and through the lateral slit of her dress she shows her white bra, which perhaps is the sign of bourgeois status. (In the country, it seems to me that a bra is a rare luxury.) We have been waiting to leave for two hours now.

34 The problem with whites is that they stimulate the hunting instinct, perhaps because of their pallor, and you become prey like the gazelles on the desert. Since yesterday evening, I've had this image of the attack on prey, aside from the vultures of the Kananga. For example, we have discovered that to go to Bandiagara, the locals pay 1000 CFA, and we pay 2000. On top of it, they proposed we spend another 4000 if we wanted to leave earlier. But I'm not in a hurry . . . One o'clock. Now we realize the misunderstanding, because in reality, everyone pays the same price, it's just people who pay less get off sooner. Two Toucouleur boys sitting on the back on the hitch act like they're on a field trip, they whisper things into each other's ears, then giggle like little girls. The one dressed in the white of the *hajji* never talks to anyone. The two German *toubabs* have Tuareg *chéches* to protect them from the dust. We're well packed in in the open-air van. Signs on the street: VIDEO CLUB, TOP ELEGANCE, ETERNELLE BEAUTÉ, OUSMANA GUITTEYE, Commerce Général, Import-Export. Jean, his child's beach hat. We exit through an imperial triumphant arch. City that enchants me.

35 I will remember the Mopti-Bandiagara trip for a while. We left with fourteen, there were only fourteen seats. Then there were twenty-five of us, plus those on the footboards on the sides, three with one leg in and hanging onto the luggage rack, and four thrust inside the driver's booth. You come to understand why this poor excuse for a vehicle had to stop every five kilometers for lack of water: it perspired like we did in the awful heat. The dust so dense that you could not breathe. I couldn't even look out at the landscape. Jean's sunhat turned the color of a brick. Everyone covered his face, I had a scarf up to my nose. But I felt a communal thread with strangers squeezed together, all of us exposed together to the desert dust. We arrived in Bandiagara, utterly exhausted, late afternoon. Everything all mixed up. The world is a big misunderstanding; no, Jean says, it is a mistake. For this reason, it pursues us or it escapes us, we are pushed here and there by having heard about things said about places, about destinations, about desires, but in essence, running after only that which is not well understood. Our situation in Bandiagara. I write with the flashlight. We're going to bed.

THIRD NOTEBOOK

1 Bandiagara. This morning Jean went to the Center for Traditional Medicine. The director, Doctor Diakité, would not see him. I have no desire to set foot ever again in that place after having gotten off the bush taxi and immediately having been taken in charge by three boys who had us walk two kilometers, packs on back, only to be then sent back by the caretaker Téodore who was wearing a cowboy hat. The same caretaker who said on the phone that they were expecting two people, the rooms were ready, and since those people could clearly only be us, the whole thing is very unclear . . . At the same moment we arrived at the bus plaza, a swarm of boys and youths glued themselves to us, three in particular who talked nonstop. One is Samou, young intellectual, the other is Abou, Dogon musician, the third is Boubou, qualified tourist guide. We wandered around wearing our backpacks. Walking in sand when so loaded down was exhausting, but that fellow Boubou insisted anyway on showing me his certificate for being a tourist guide. Jean, who is constantly needing to eat and drink, wanted to have a Coca-Cola, he couldn't fight the urge. The three boys took us to a bar, a *buvette*, that is to say a courtyard of sand with four walls made of *banko*. You come all this way and you see that kids do the same things everywhere, if they can't get together in tribal bands and secret societies, they hang out in a bar listening to American music at the highest possible volume. Hard to have a conversation because of the din. But Jean insisted on approaching the locals, and Samou contributed a great deal as an enthusiastic talker. While I asked myself where we would be sleeping, Samou went into an enthusiastic oration on writers. Then the discussion drifted to working together with whites as an interpreter, and to the fact that his name is written in a white man's book, I don't know which one. "To have worked with whites" is a qualification to which he attaches a great deal of significance. Boubou would, as well, and he kept wanting to show me his certificate as a tourist guide, while Abou thinks only about his music, which is of an American type with insertions of Dogon rhythms, as I understand it.

2 Evening in a house in the country. The dog, the cat, Jean's lecture to me because I didn't comport myself well with the three Dogon kids: I did not present myself as a serious European writer. But here, above anything else, I am a white-skinned phantom, lost tourist, what else can I say. It's too easy to act like writers who go to exotic countries with very advanced ideas, forgetting that they are whites and tourists. In the dark, I explained the thing to Jean, I even quoted Shakespeare to him. Up until Mopti, it was thrilling because it was a situation of being in transit, whereas this is a place where everything is set.

3 Story heard by Samou. He was talking about that Dogon writer whose spirit was stolen in France and he went crazy, because the French were envious and they couldn't stand that he was extremely intelligent, Samou says, so therefore they stole his spirit from him and he now lives in Sévaré and if he sees a white person he flies into a rage. Abou explained the mental conditions of this writer, joking about it, he's not an intellectual who makes a great tragedy of things. But questions of insanity are the order of the day in these parts. Jean says that Coppo told him about many kids who run away from their families, go to Bamako on foot, then in Bamako, away from their families, they go crazy, because their spirits and minds are stolen in the city, and then they have to be brought home and cured by the Dogon healers. It seems that the first sign of insanity manifests itself as rage and insults against the father. In the name of the father, we go mad.

4 A pair of structures behind us, there in front a small fortress which they say is inhabited by Germans, and then an indefinite expanse of land as far as the first houses of Bandiagara, which are a half-kilometer away. The villa where we're staying (three domes that look like *trulli,* like those at the Center for Traditional Medicine) is Dr. Coppo's villa. The day before, as soon as we got off at Bandiagara, those kids started asking us right away, "Do you know Piero Coppo?" And Jean made a good impression, saying he knew him very well and that he was the reason we had come. But then they wouldn't stop talking about Coppo, the founder of the Center for Medicine, who's supposed to arrive in Bandiagara very soon. Everyone knew everything, but you can't understand anything. Dr. Diakité, to whom we sent faxes and letters, has not yet been seen, and they keep telling us he's not there. Upon our arrival at the Center for Medicine, the caretaker Téodore sent us to Coppo's house, in the exact opposite part of the city, without giving us any explanations. Bewildered, we came here, where Amadou greeted us with the face of someone at a complete loss about what he should do . . .

5 Amadou doesn't want me to wash the dishes, he doesn't want me to do the laundry, he wants to do it all himself, however, he always has a few second thoughts that trouble him. A beautiful face, a beautiful green suit that is almost sumptuous which he puts on again every evening to go home, intense eyes that are often mournful, darting here and there . . . At the table he talks to us about the languages he knows. There are forty-eight Dogon dialects, he knows five of them. He was even in Italy and for this reason they call him Amadou the Italian here. He likes to tell stories, he is proud of having been adopted by Coppo. He watches over the house and tends the garden. The garden is his favorite place and he spends time here, he goes home to his wife only in the evening. When he is alone, he feels like the master of the house, in which case he takes catnaps in the afternoon. Before us, there was a Brazilian anthropologist here whom he talks about often. He acted as interpreter for her. She sends him an anthropological bulletin in Portuguese, which Amadou certainly does not understand, but which he shows to me as if it were a precious gift.

6 Jean has still not succeeded in meeting with Dr. Diakité to talk to him about the documentary. One might say that our arrival has irritated him, given that he sent us away without explanation, while the guest quarters at the center are empty, according to Amadou. We read, sleep, chat in this bunker cut off from the world. Ever since we arrived in Bandiagara my grand visions have collapsed, precisely from the moment I set foot in that Center for Traditional Medicine. A center created by Italians, designed by an Italian architect. I immediately sniffed out the atmosphere of the place. That center is a Local Health Authority, which they have transplanted here in the savanna.

7 During the night after Amadou went home, we kept talking and smoking in the thick darkness, drinking a type of *carcadé* that Amadou made for us, as the concert of dogs under the stars flared up even more; it was a barking competition where they all got more worked up hearing the others. The collective barking took on a jerky rhythm, and after one long howl you heard something like an outburst of coughing, and our house dog wanted to join the others who were barking with coughs. For this reason, when we went to bed we could not sleep, because every now and then he started up again, too, with that cough in order to make contact with the other dogs. I had to go out and yell at him, after which he stopped, only to start up again as soon as we had fallen back to sleep.

8 This morning we went to the post office with Amadou, crossing through nondescript land outside the city to avoid

governess as a child. On the other hand, his melancholy around seven-thirty in the evening, usually at the end of dinner, stirs up in us a certain extra affection for our Amadou.

10 Night begins about six-thirty, seven, the sky becomes whitish, there's an absolute silence, and we eat chatting outside without mosquitoes. Around eight you start to hear voices from the neighborhoods a kilometer away, with no light whatsoever on the horizon because there is no electricity here. You hear the beating of a gong at the wind-powered pump for pulling water out of the river, and scattered and intermittent voices, mostly of little girls' giggling. Then, toward night, music, perhaps from some radio or tape recorder, and little by little still another crescendo of high-pitched female voices that give the sense of a party, together with the braying of an ass coming from behind us. From here, we see only some glowing flickers of flames coming from parts of the nearest neighborhood, but we hear clapping and singing as if they were having a party, even though it's an ordinary day. Because at the end of the day, people get together to talk, to sing, to laugh. We know nothing about these get-togethers, we ask ourselves where they're taking place, whether in the courtyards, in the street, or just where. Only later do we hear the sounds of television, a forceful male voice making a speech. And still more outbursts of children's laughter, on the background of a shrill female voice singing to the sound of a flute. Night comes, listening like this, and when the voices cease, you hear the barking of the dogs, a few brays of a lonely donkey, the moaning of a cat in heat. But above all in the nondescript land that separates us from the neighborhood, still more baying of dogs starting up again, they reply and whimper and give long howls, from one part of the savanna to the other. In the meanwhile, the sky is completely cleansed, the dust has settled to the ground, and the view of the stars is very different from the one of our faded skies, with bundles of constellations I do not know. One would need a map of the African sky to recognize the symmetrical clusters that shine above, chains of constellations that expand in the east, while in the west, the sky is emptier.

11 A little after our arrival, the neighbor from the garden next door came in to say hello to us, and later he came back bringing his baby boy. Amadou called him his "cousin," however, after the third visit he told us that it would be better if we didn't talk to him or get too friendly with him. "Fine." The next day, however, the neighbor came back bringing us one of his friends who sells Dogon statuettes and barely speaks French, and today this statuette vendor showed up alone. I could not get it through his head that we didn't want statuettes, thus I had to seek out Amadou. Naturally, right after this, Amadou began his complaint: that we do not listen to him and we do not understand how things work around here. ("I warn you, but you do not listen.") This goes back to his role as a local expert who points out our errors to us, because here everything must fall in with a collective music, where one cannot be off-key. But by dint of taking care of whites, I would say that Amadou is isolated from the collective music, and now he has a foot in one world, one foot in another, that is to say, a very uncomfortable position. The only thing that gives him peace is taking refuge in this garden, in seclusion, perhaps content to have found two other recluses who can share his isolation.

12 A fax arrived from Thomas Harlan, via the German doctor friend of Amadou. In this fax he commands Jean to verify everything needed to make the documentary: (1) electricity (which there isn't here), (2) places to sleep for the troupe and the entourage of twenty or so people (impossible to lodge so many people here), (3) transportation and the cost of it (it would be necessary to go to Mopti to find out), (4) prices of hotels and restaurants (which ones?). Jean is there on his bed under the mosquito netting, mulling over all of this. I don't know what to tell him.

13 Yesterday evening a meeting with the aristocrat of the place, the young Amadou Ouoleghem, scion of the family of Bandiagara's founders. Our own Amadou is a descendant of the same stock, but he's poor while the other seems rich by local standards. And it is this young Ouoleghem who has all the ceremonial signs of the old African nobility, aside from the fact that he coaches a soccer team. He received us in his bar, a courtyard with four tables covered with straw canopies, sand on the ground and uncomfortable benches, completely empty. He sat there in the shade, drinking beer from a liter bottle and exchanging complex discourses on ceremonial representation, seasoned with explanations about his estate, which, in truth, was hardly ostentatious. Above all, it was I, curious about where his elevated status originates, about his aristocratic insouciance, who asked questions, as he called the waiter over to bring us another beer every once in a while. Each time he returned to sit down with us, he told us about his welcome to Bandiagara and why they always called him to manage some matter or another, to settle some question at home or on the street. From this vantage point, one made note of his importance, as well as his courteous way of expressing his pleasure talking to us, a little as if we were visiting his court. He carried himself beautifully, a tall, thin youth in a Lacoste tee shirt, serious and reserved face, sober in his speech, but with an open and adolescent smile.

14 There is an old Dogon man at the garden door who is talking in Dogon with Jean. Jean repeats every word and says that he does not understand. They stand there looking at each other, neither one of the two can find a way to communicate. Then we talk about leaving for the high plain of the Dogon villages, but first it's necessary to resolve the situation of the money, which is being depleted. The only hope is Coppo's arrival, awaited from one day to the next in Bandiagara. In the streets, everyone is asking each other: "When's Coppo arriving?" His name is even on the lips of the children. Dr. Diakité has still not seen Jean.

15 The young aristocrat Ouoleghem invited us to the baptism of the daughter of one of his Ouoleghem relatives, where we went today. A courtyard like all the others, among the little alleyways, houses of mud which seemed a little ramshackle to me. We were welcomed by someone who was really quite muscular, the flashy smile of a Latin lover, speaking to us in Spanish because he had heard that we were Italian. This was the famous antiquarian Antonio, whose real name was Ante Temely, of Bandiagara's second founding family. Gathering with the men to chat in the courtyard after the baptism while waiting for the noonday meal, the *gros repas de midi,* and the music of the tape recorder which was frankly annoying. The young men had shaved heads, like the kids in the American ghetto, one with Rasta dreadlocks, and they all sat on a bench sloppily dressed. And finally I met the first *griot* ever in my life, after having heard a great deal said about these African storytellers who preserve the tribal genealogy. He had come to the baptism in order to proclaim the ancient origins and the descent of the noble Ouoleghem of Bandiagara. A dried-out old man, a head that was round like a billiard ball, white caftan, small angry eyes, he raised his voice to speak conventional phrases about the nobility, money, women, just so everyone would listen to him patiently. So, later, when he said something to me with a stentorian tone, I had no response (and he was truly dislikable to me because of his shouted preaching), and after he began speaking with the others, he started to mock whites. He yelled about those who come here and do not know anything, then want to write books on the life of the Dogon without knowing anything about it, and he angrily dwelled upon our ignorance as if he were a high school principal. It was clear that he took us for anthropologists, and turning his back to us he started shouting in French so that we would perfectly understand his sarcasms. We were all sitting there on the little benches in the courtyard, and one could hear only his rancorous voice. There was one near me who was dressed in European clothing, in the style of a small-town official, who was having a great time listening to all these insults against whites. The young people with American cuts, on the other hand, listened to the *griot* with great annoyance. The young aristocrat Ouoleghem came over to bring us sweets from the baptism and to tell us that he very much enjoyed our chat the other evening, adding that he wanted to get together with us again as soon as possible for another little chat with us, a "petit bavardage." It was as if an ancient African sovereign had expressed satisfaction with our presence, with beautiful manners, very ceremonial, but also with the ease of a boarding school mate. I liked him a lot, and as we parted we made plans to get together again.

16 In the morning we find ourselves once again caught up in the network of contracts, of assignments, which has held us in its grip since the moment we arrived. I have in mind the evening in which Samou talked to us about the writer who lives in Sévaré and cannot see a white person without going insane. The discussion was about a book of this writer, and Jean had asked if someone in Bandiagara has a copy of it. From that moment, without knowing it, we entered into complicated negotiations in order to read the book. Because as soon as they heard this, the others responded: ah, that book interests you? fine, we'll look for it for you. And you enter into a situation of promises, with all the consequences. Namely, it is implicitly understood that if Samou takes on looking for that book, it means that it is a job that requires compensation because of the fact that books are not easily found in Bandiagara. This is also the meaning of presenting oneself as someone who "has worked a great deal with whites" (the same thing Amadou brags about), because it is understood that looking for that book means engaging in a specific profession called "working with whites." A profession that goes from acting as an interpreter for anthropologists to acting as a tourist guide, but in between there is everything else, including finding a bicycle for Jean, bringing whites to the market, and maybe even finding him a woman, who knows. In any case, if you say here: "I want, I would like, I would like it if," then afterwards you can't think about the thing you have said as if it were just the whim of a distracted European. In a few hours, through the grapevine, it instead becomes a public call throughout the city. In fact, this morning Samou introduced us to a guy who would find the book of this writer from Sévaré and would be willing to make a photocopy of it for us. But the negotiations are difficult because we can't settle on how much a photocopy of a book would cost in Bandiagara. Amadou, like a maternal governess, urges us to think hard about it, because afterwards we will have to pay something for the labor of having found the book, etc.

17 This evening Amadou gave us an exceptional performance, reciting stories like African theater, cases of adultery and magical vendetta, seduced women, hunters of the savanna, avenging husbands, questions of kinships, terrible homicides. We didn't understand anything, but he is a true actor. The idea of putting aside the documentary on the Center for Medicine emerged, thinking instead about a documentary put together this way: invite our storytellers here, who would recount magical and fantastic stories, together with local storytellers like Amadou, and have a festival of stories on the savanna, between richly laden tables and huge fires. Crazy ideas of recluses. However, the point is this: Amadou keeps us captive with his arts as a sorcerer, because every moment he invents another one, and we never get bored with him, through good and bad. Even though Jean cannot stand his role as our nanny.

18 Another surprise by our Amadou, who every so often launches into telling us stories like African theater, or who knows what they are. For example: the story of a hunter who while hunting learns through his magical powers that his wife has been betraying him, and so he flies back home as a spirit and kills his rival. The idea that came to Jean, to record these stories, keeping in mind as well that Amadou likes his beer, had an unexpected outcome. After supper, we went to have some beers at the *buvette* of our aristocrat Ouoleghem, still empty, where our Amadou immediately drank a liter without pausing. But when we asked him to tell us a story, he all of a sudden got mad, replying that one doesn't speak about certain things in public. He made us feel like barbarians who do not understand good African manners, and we were almost ashamed. Then I thought about it again, and in the dark I saw the profile of another Amadou . . . In our chatting at home, he lets himself go with laughs, sadness, confessions about his marital life, laments about his poverty, in addition to stories where he probably invented everything. The theatrical African stories that he tells us, I think he invents on the spot, as he invents many other things just to talk. For example, when we asked him the number of people who live in Bandiagara, he replied with the first number that came into his head, a stunningly bad error. With us, he always says the first thing that pops into his head, and he's happy this way, for this reason he very happily talks. But in public there is a different Amadou, which you could see at the baptism of his Ouoleghem relative. In public he assumes a distant air, he becomes "Amadou the Italian," Coppo's right hand, the serious and reserved man, who does not mix with his fellow countrymen. And he would never let himself be caught in a *buvette,* selling himself out with his fanciful inventions to two whites who aren't even anthropologists. An astonishing person, of multiple humanity, who can fold himself up back into himself. I would listen forever to this enchanter.

19 Bandiagara attracts me a great deal, but we are trapped in this bunker, surrounded by the garden walls that keep us sheltered, separated from the city by a half-kilometer of emptiness. Dr. Diakité still has not seen Jean, who has become deflated insofar as his cinematographic enthusiasm is concerned. The idea of a documentary on the Center for Traditional Medicine has come to nothing. I forget about everything else writing my notes about the trip. How long have we been here? It seems like a lifetime, in our comfortable colonial bunker.

20 For years anthropologists and psychiatrists have been coming here to study the methods of the Dogon healers at the Center for Traditional Medicine. Constructed with Italian cooperation with Mali, according to the vision (I think) of Piero Coppo who had lived in Bandiagara for more than ten years, this center is now famous throughout the world. Now I think that the Italians only exported their concept of the Local Health Authority, with the variation of Dogon methods put into official practice. The center is a series of semispherical brick domes, said to be inspired by a local style. For this reason, they're called "nonintrusive architecture," Jean explains to me. But these round things make me think of an indiscriminate African exoticism, lost in the harsh reality of the industrial brick of mass construction. That is to say, a true Local Health Authority in the savanna . . . At the center there is a director (Dr. Diaketé) and two doctors: one is devoted to general medicine, the other to psychiatric cures. Each time I have gone to the center it has been completely empty, except for the lady working at the computer (who turned out to be Dr. Diakité's wife), Téodore the watchman with the cowboy hat, and the driver who was snoozing. The patients are not in-patients so they come to get medicine or have treatments, then they go back home. Strange, however, that the animation of African life, the rhythms according to the hours of the day, are not in evidence here at all. They seem abolished. It is the deadest place we have visited, where one breathes in the heavy air of bureaucratic illness, as if they have imposed the humiliation of the timecard even upon sick people, so they can accumulate a quantity of interviews and documentation about the Dogon healers in the archives which will be something useful to academics, anthropologists, psychiatrists. But it is, as well, the supreme exploit of state-inspired abstractions: "to make culture," creating places without cheerfulness like enforcement agencies, located even in the savanna.

21 In the morning Amadou waits in the chair until we wake up. He always says he has been waiting since six, that he gets up at five to go buy bread, and this puts him in the role of a poor black man in the service of whites. It's a role that he likes to play, even as he acts as our caretaker. The other role that he likes is that of the public relations man: knowing our financial difficulties, he says we will go with him to Mopti, and they will accept our credit cards because they know him very well in the banks there. ("I have a lot of connections, they know me everywhere.") Lastly, he likes the role of the administrator, with the ledger books of accounts in the cupboard, and in the evening, after supper, he starts to calculate in a loud voice the purchases he has to make the next day. We do not understand anything about it, but he writes numbers, then the performance is finished and he goes home. He is like an actor who can't stay inside a role because he needs to interpret many, always with passion and conviction. The anthropologists never take into account these performances, nor of the fact that we all perform in order to pretend to be ourselves. They immediately eliminate this theater of encounters, which produces emotions, likes and dislikes, in addition to a large quantity of fanciful stories. They take in everything as information, said as fact, conceptual explanations. In this way, interpretive mimicking, which is very human, which is Amadou's great ability, becomes a kind of folkloric option of the indigenous informer . . . On the other hand, Amadou likes his anthropologists a lot, without reserve he loves the whites he has worked with, because they have changed his life. He speaks about them with eyes lighting up, conscious of his merits, standing at attention: "Amadou the Italian, interpreter-guide, one hundred percent Bandiagarois!"

22 Morning in the garden. Birds with long tails and a shrill cry, which seems like a razzing of whoever is listening. Amadou, in his undershirt, cleans his teeth with the little wooden stick taken from a tree called the *nime,* and he's carrying on the same conversation that I heard one time in the piazza from one of our charlatans, who proclaimed that brushing teeth with a toothbrush ruins the enamel, therefore it was necessary to use the small stick like the Africans. Breakfast is ready . . . Before going out, Jean wants to take a picture of Amadou in his beautiful green tunic. Amadou immediately lowers his eyebrows, striking a pose as if he is considering something extremely interesting, like a person who sees and understands the seriousness of a situation. But as soon as Jean goes *click,* his face completely changes, showing that smile of his of a boy on an outing, who loves beer and potatoes. I am always struck by the transformism of his face, and I would say that by virtue of having been with whites Amadou has become a great actor. A splendid mediator between different modes of living, due to his enthusiasm for theatrical performance. I don't think I'm showing disrespect for him in writing these notes, but I suppose that whites find him a little bit of a brown-noser and that they are pleased with him.

23 With all this organizing of the meal schedule, of shopping budgets, of going to buy things, which Amadou manages like clockwork, it's ended up that the center of our life is here and I still haven't seen Bandiagara as I would like. We cross through it always at a sprint. I don't even know how big it is, and I am unable to distinguish its inhabitants, Dogon, Toucouleur, etc. . . . One very large main street, completely of sand, little houses made of mortarless brickwork, each one with a courtyard, then the small modern villa of the German doctor. The little shops, in the absence of other written advertisements, display the flashy Marlboro poster. After the big intersection, where the piazza for the buses is, one loses oneself in the side streets in incredibly narrow zigzagging lanes, with the pavement full of bumps and sandy holes. Here, there are older houses made of *banko* which are falling down, where Amadou took me today. Most of all, I'm attracted to the life of the courtyards: one low door, arch made of clay and straw, which gives into a squared space with three or four dwelling places, where you frequently see tied-up goats, a dog wandering around, hung-out sheets, babies left to themselves. Someone arrives on a moped, a baby sifting through who-knows-what, a woman pounding the *fonio.* All of these daily goings-on in the courtyard are like time suspended, and the lovely colors of the clothing are a halo around the life of pure subsistence.

24 Today Amadou pointed out to me the door of a Dogon healer who cures the insane, but he said that the healer is more insane than the ones he cures. I said that it's like that even with our psychiatrists, and I asked him if he would introduce me. But he hurried away without wanting to listen to me, reissuing his warning, his technical assessment, about that healer. ("He's crazy, he's crazy.") I suspect, as well, that from hanging around psychiatrists Amadou considers himself qualified to diagnose the mental condition of his neighbors . . . But today he irritated me with his anxiety about going back to the house and being isolated from people, always closed up in that garden as if in perpetual service. Luckily afterwards he made a side trip to take me to see how millet beer is made, and we passed by the courtyard of a lady who comes from the Ivory Coast. She was cooking the millet in a huge pot, but dressed as if she were going to a party, and she spoke magnificent French, with long drawn-out phrases, extraordinarily self-possessed, gestures without expedience, countenance without a trace of distrust. I would never get tired of looking at her, I would have even courted her just to be able to stay there chatting with her in that courtyard. But Amadou was in a hurry, she invited us to come back when the beer was ready.

25 And if I were to stay and live in Bandiagara? An idea that came to me tonight. Every morning I would take a stroll saying hello to the people that I know at this point, or even those I don't know, in order to see the colors that stand out in the skittering light. For example, the light in the courtyards, the shadows in the little shops, the red of the Marlboro advertisement, the facade of the government palace, with clay that lightens up in the morning until it becomes nearly pink. Then a stroll in the afternoon, around four, when everyone remains in the protection of the long shadows, conversations on the street are scarce, the sand is scorching, even the dogs don't go out for a walk, but one is comfortable in the little side streets, even in the cool *buvette*, between the *banko* walls and winding corners, where everyone gladly greets you. Then, evening is irresistible, beginning at six-thirty, with the big evening stroll and the mixing of every type on the main street. The oldest stay off to the side watching, while the young people walk around exploring in bands, and strange figures from the *brousse* appear (like the one yesterday who was dressed in leather, bandolier slung over his shoulder, long hair, eyes of a madman, who looked like Robinson Crusoe). After this hour there is a slow mutation of rhythms, of strides, of the ways of talking, where all the vivacity seems to have died down, but it's not true. It starts up again in other keys around eight, around nine, around ten . . .

26 After the walk to the post office (without Jean who went back in search of Dr. Diakité), we passed by the weekly market. A marvel to look at for hours, but Amadou is always in a hurry to get back home . . . Going to the post office, we met the marabout, the Muslim holy man, who is exactly like our parish priest. Busy, on a moped, he hands out consolatory words hurriedly ("Courage . . ."), then he goes off like our priests. At the post office, the head clerk is identical to our postal clerks, that is to say birdbrained but having to prove they're important. We had a squabble over my telephone call, because I had hung up the phone without giving them warning (the line was cut off), and he assumed the unmistakable functionary-lecturing tone of our government employees. By contrast, in the office of the German cooperative organization, that young Malian director, who was so gentle, was like one of my pals from high school. He said he had completed the École Normale Supérieure, had studied literature but doesn't know with whom he can talk about it, so he would like it if we could meet, as a kind of educational get-together. The longer I stay here, the more I seem to see everywhere roles that I know, behaviors that remind me of something. It is as if all of man's secrets were exposed in the open, in the general functioning of daylight, in the performances everyone must make in order to be who he is. That's why in the end one can simply say: "That's life." Now, what's come to mind is the weekly market I saw today: festival of the most usual things in the world, between women who display their little heaps of oranges, cloth vendors who call you to come back, ladies who go shopping in their best dresses, chatting, drums, kola nuts and tires.

27 Before supper, I watched the butchering of the chicken. Amadou recited a short verse from the Koran to prevent the spirit of the chicken from producing evil effects. He likes to give these explanations, but then he happily drinks beer because he says he is a "civilized Muslim" . . . The three of us closed up in the bunker for whites, everything else seems like a sound on the horizon, students' voices from the public school carried by the wind. Jean does not know what to do or think anymore about his documentary. I write or read, this is enough for me. Amadou has to transcribe a cassette of interviews for the Brazilian anthropologist, who is writing her doctoral dissertation on the Dogon. During the night, a very strong wind, hard to sleep underneath the mosquito netting with the drafts.

28 Word has spread that we want to go to the high plain to the Dogon villages, and this evening a young man came to offer his services as a guide, in reality called by Amadou who is his relative. The interesting thing is that this Boubacar Ouoleghem is cited in the travel guide *Lonely Planet,* and it's surprising to find ourselves with a celebrity at supper by candlelight. He immediately declares that he is the most expensive guide, and we sit down at the table with this announcement. He is twenty-five years old, sober and aloof, cultured (we spoke about Marcel Griaule's work), he keeps his distance from us. I asked him what he wants to do in the future, given that he is already so famous. He says he would like to start up a travel agency, to organize pirogue trips between Gao and Mopti and Timbuktu, but he also says that he does not want to fantasize too much. He just does not want to work for travel agencies with owners because, with them, there is no distinction between one guide and another; when it comes down to it, one is as good as the other for looking after the *toubabs*. While he is different from the others—this, in a nutshell, is what he's saying. Self-assured type, better this way. (Usually people who are unsure of themselves become too much of a burden while traveling.)

29 We're waiting for the arrival of Dr. Coppo, who should be able to resolve our financial problems as well as others, we hope. We should leave for the high plain of the Dogon Sunday morning with some Belgian tourists, according to the plans of our guide, Boubacar. More than the trek from village to village, I am curious about the Belgian tourists. I am rereading Griaule's book, and I get lost in the explanations about this immense cosmology of the Dogon, which has everything descending from the stars, as if we, by contrast, live blindly under the sky, unfortunates with no memory, full of information, closed off by the horizon line of events . . .

30 Among the textbook cases of African tourism, it would be necessary to make note of those that concern scholars, psychiatrists, functionaries of European cooperative ventures, and a whole fringe group of white individuals who arrive here, pick up something, make good money and go back home. In any event, one textbook case is that of the Parisian psychiatrist who came here to study the healing methods of the Dogon, now in Paris curing mental illnesses with Dogon magic; he has great worldly success, and to top it off, he has written a detective novel of a Dogon mystery set in Paris, stuff to be ashamed of for an eternity, but now they're making a film as well.

31 Amadou said that Coppo arrives today. Very much on pins and needles, he has figured out all the things we have to buy to prepare him a lovely dinner. The morning went on in this way, Jean has gone shopping with Amadou . . . Yesterday evening on a walk at sunset, a woman sitting in the street greeted me in a French so broken that I could not understand. I approached her and she was speaking in English, she comes from Nigeria. She seemed cheered up by exchanging a few words, even if we didn't understand each other much. We were two foreigners in the middle of a street, without a place where we could go to talk, in reality, without anything to say to each other. But everything was slow, very much dragging, with an inertia with the power to induce sleep while we waited for a word to come out of our mouths. I had the taste of everyday life, which wasn't going anywhere, and remained suspended like a cloud above a gorge. That's why journeys get you drunk right away, one becomes accustomed to the excitement of drifting, then it seems that life must be going somewhere ... At the door to the garden, there's a guy with a yellow towel on his head who wants to sell me kola nuts.

FOURTH NOTEBOOK

1 Twelve o'clock. We're up on the high plain. A stop at the first village, Dourou; in the courtyard of a house, we're stretched out in the shade of a straw hut. This village isn't made like a Dogon village, it's only a clearing with four brick houses, another one under construction, and it must be an outpost on the cliff. You can't walk around between noon and three because the sun beats down too hard, and so I have time to write. Yesterday afternoon, my stinginess suddenly vanished. A huge car arrived, Amadou went outside and immediately we heard a whining sound, it wasn't clear whether it was laughter or crying, interrupted by curt replies in a white man's voice. We went out to see. A very tall white man appeared, he was distinguished in an English-gentleman kind of way, followed by two dwarf anthropologists dressed in safari clothes. They told us that we needed to get ourselves over to the Center for Traditional Medicine, this instant, not a moment to lose, the reason wasn't clear. Amadou was struck dumb, his eyes darting from person to person . . . After being chased away from Coppo's house, Jean is a little dazed; I, instead, can go on in my usual idiot's contentment. We will never understand how things work here. We had even prepared a lovely dinner, which was then eaten by that fellow who arrived with the two anthropologists. However, driving us away produced some good, including an evening away from the bunker, the end of my stinginess, and the decision to leave with our guide Boubacar right away.

2 Five kilometers from Bandiagara everything changes. The people speak only local dialects, old villages are scattered across a scrubland, the road is full of holes. We passed near a village called Pelou, where the antiquarian Antonio (Ante Temely) says his ancestors lived, and last evening he told us how the old people there spend their lives drunk on millet beer because this is how they have their visions . . . Now a German traveler has arrived, a blond; a hasty greeting, we don't talk. The surprise is that the German is crossing the high plain without a guide, in the company of a young fellow from Papua New Guinea who has a grim face and a big machete in his backpack. The young man from Papua New Guinea is eating honey fritters brought over by a little girl, and he sniffs them and studies them one by one with a nearsighted gaze before putting them into his mouth. The little girl is spellbound watching the strange spectacle. Of course, there is the danger of ingesting parasites by eating the food up here; still, our hygienic preoccupations are enough to make someone laugh, Boubacar, for example, who masterfully kidded us this morning: Yes, yes. The parasites make you ill, but for us, it's like protein.

3 I doze off leaning against the wall. The Papuan with the nearsighted glasses doesn't confide in anyone, he doesn't respond to the lively banter, he's irritated because they mistook him for a Japanese. To make conversation, Jean asks him something about the Bay of Astrolabio in his faraway land. Meanwhile, Boubacar is looking at the notebook of a little boy who attends elementary school in Dourou; he notes the errors, gives grammatical advice. This morning he left with a cap made out of indigo cloth, which rises up from the ears into a triangle, with small pom-poms at the lateral angles. It is the Dogon cap designated for his age, and there are eight caps among the Dogon, according to the stage of life. I take notes like a student on a field trip, it's my state of mind.

4 The climb up the escarpment with a backpack is fairly difficult, but up until this point it's been like a hike in the country. You make the ascent by stepping from stone to stone, heading toward the ridge of the high plain, which then descends sharply on the other side, where the desert is. Boubacar climbs among the stones and sandstone rocks as if he knows each one individually, already knowing which is the best path, the one that will make the climb easier . . . Crumbling synclines; it seems like the mountain is breaking into pieces. Pinkish faults are streaked across the sides of the mountain's back, and between the faults longitudinal fissures open up, the places where the Tellem lived before the arrival of the Dogon. How they managed to live up there in perpendicular rock is unimaginable to us. Jean tries to photograph one of those fissures in the wall.

5 Up until this point, we haven't met anyone. At the most beautiful point from the top of the cliffs, we see a rock ridge in front of us that looks like wrinkled elephant's skin and almost has the roundness of an elephant's back. Then, over on the other side is the desert of sand, which extends all the way to the border of Burkina Faso. Dunes made of very red sand, with a few scattered little trees down below the cliffs, and then sand as far as the eye can see. A beautiful example of desertification, as Boubacar says, of how, for example, Timbuktu is under siege, of how the water resources above Gao are being wiped out, which is forcing the Tuareg to move from the Algerian border toward the south, and how, for this reason, northern Mali is nearly in a state of war . . . Thinking about it again during a break on the Bandiagara Cliffs: that man must have had good reason to drive us away from the house in such a hurry, aside from putting the dwarf anthropologists in our beds. Upon our arrival, Dr. Diakité had given the order to send us to Coppo's house because we were here under Coppo's protection, but maybe that order was a hostile gesture directed at Coppo, maybe there's a secret war against the Center for Traditional Medicine, and for this reason, every move is part of a preexisting field of tension which we were dropped right into the middle of. Still, I don't understand why he and the two anthropologists ate our dinner.

6 We're in a Dogon village but my ears are ringing and I didn't catch the name. When it appeared off in the distance, rising up from a gorge, it reminded me of one of those farms you see in Puglia because of the low wall that surrounds it. Six-thirty. I want to eat and sleep. You can't go wandering around the little streets of the village; we must stay in the *case de passage*, a travelers' shelter, which is below the village. Boubacar told us this in a lowered voice, suggesting that respectful behavior is essential up here. Actually, this village is one of a nucleus of three scattered on a ridge around a peak, but I don't know where the other two are. The village is formed in an oval, and it seems to me that it coincides with Griaule's description, even though Boubacar says that now very few Dogon villages are laid out in the form of a human body, with head, legs, arms, on a north-south axis (the writer Griaule's description).

7 A low wall made of stones and mud-brick surrounds the oval shape of the village. At the northwest end is the so-called *case de palabre*, where the elders gather. It is a long portico made of wooden posts, with eight thin layers of straw on top, but one cannot stand upright underneath it, and I deduce that when the elders gather to decide about public matters they lie on the ground, perhaps drunk on millet beer. This is an idea suggested by Ante Telemy, but Boubacar does not confirm it. At any rate, outside the wall, halfway down the oval on the east side, is the house where menstruating women stay. From there, there's a little path from which they cannot veer, so that they don't spread around their impurity. At the south end, outside the oval, behind us, is the temple, which has a very dark facade which I can see very little of from here. The *case de passage* where travelers stop is at the extreme southern part of the village. Its construction is more or less cubical, mud and straw like all the others; in front there is a canopy covered with straw, under which the seats where we are resting are in an open space. A family runs the *case de passage*, the husband has just come back and shook our hands. The wife is preparing food in tins on the ground, little girls are helping her, going back and forth into the house, and all around chickens are pecking at the ground. We will sleep on the roof.

8 Coming toward Djiguibombo on an irregular plain with a few bushes, we were very high up, and you could see only sky, it was like looking at a floor upside down, with stripes and bands low on the edge that signaled sunset, everything to the west was still. Later, whitish bands formed a triangle on a red background, and the bands suspended in air were so deep, a depth far beyond the ordinary. Today we walked for eight hours. Evening. It starts to get dark at seven. Silence throughout the village, the only voices are those of the children in the *case de passage*. In front of us, the Dogon granaries make up nearly three-quarters of the village. Striking in the half-light, dark pyramids made of mud, like a cosmologic image of the blacksmith's mallet coming down from the sky to bring water and fire to men, and contained within compartments of the granary are seeds from the eight original sowings. The granary of the husband is coupled with that of the wife, as husband and wife should be coupled in bed. A little opening in sculpted wood is reminiscent of a mouth, two iron spikes above form the eyes. In reality, they are masks that recall the original couple, I would say. But this place is hardly exotic; there is an austerity so total that it brings on a desire to remain immobile like the granaries.

9 Slept heavily, even though I was cold in the sleeping bag. Seen from outside, from the slope, this village seems like a shapeless mass of houses, granaries, patched chunks of wall. The granaries stand out, each with a roof similar to the straw hat

I'm wearing. They are the only buildings distinguishable from a distance, they have an air about them that is not exotic as much as rustic. I climbed up a sandstone cliff that closes off the village in the north so as to compare it to the layout of the houses described by Griaule. It is a perfect oval on a north-south axis. At the northern point, the oval should end up in the shape of the blacksmith's mallet, but there is only a little piazza here. From above, it seemed unpopulated to me. During the day, only the *hogon* remains, I think. Among all the families he is the oldest, the keeper of spiritual traditions, who remains lying because if he were to sweat it would be a disgrace. His house is more or less in the center of the village, but to see him one must have a special reason, which we tourists do not have; this is how the scrupulous Boubacar explains it to us. The lady of the *case de passage* pays us no more attention and chases the piglet out of the house. Jean has lost something. We're leaving . . .

10 I can't stop very often to write because the hike follows the sun's timetable. Boubacar calculates precisely how long it will take us to get from one point to another, even if he has no watch. His clock is his regular stepping, which is like a metronome, never an acceleration or a sudden move, a sight even more striking to me than the landscape. This morning, when I told him that his way of walking had made an impression on me, he said with detachment, "Ah, it is my art." He finds satisfaction in his work as a guide because it is an art, you can see this in his pace where everything is unforced, composed, reduced to essential movements. I suggest to Jean that he give up on the documentary on the center in Bandiagara and make one about Boubacar, his craft as a guide, his ideas, his way of walking.

11 We follow the ridge of the Bandiagara Cliffs, but from here you can't see the precipice to the southwest. We passed by an onion garden, Jean took out his camera and immediately a man stood up from a rock and started yelling. We had not seen him because he was lying down, but his prohibition against taking pictures of this ordinary place makes me think. For us, in fact, it is merely an ordinary place at the opening of a deep, narrow valley, like many others. (The fact is that a stone, a tree, a piece of land can be sacred even without looking any different from others.) During a break, I listen to Jean and Boubacar; they're talking about Dogon kids who run off to the city, then soon go out of their minds, and when they come back to the village, they have to be cured by the healer, but they aren't able to settle back down, and they have to leave again. As a matter of fact, up here I don't see any young people, only the elderly, women and children, but for me, it's impossible to determine the ages of these people.

12 I tell Jean about a story about two characters, Cevenini and Ridolfi, which came to me as I was walking. There isn't time to write all of it down ... Cevenini is half deaf, Ridolfi is blind in one eye and nearsighted in the other ... Ridolfi is very cultured and, for this reason, always has to be right and can't stand to be contradicted. So Cevenini always tells him he's right ... When they were at home, and they would go to their small-town, country bar every day, it would so happen that every three months Ridolfi would go crazy and then would break up all the furniture in the house. In his raging against being born, he would break everything, and they would have to take him to the asylum ... One day, Cevenini read in the newspaper about a famous Professor Paponio, who had erected a center for medicine in a place in Africa where they cure insanity with the magical methods of the African healers. So, he decided to take his friend Ridolfi to have him cured by magic ...

13 Evening, 5:30. The village where we are now seems to me to be the same as the other villages I have seen. What has started up now is familiarity, which makes things unremarkable, and I'm unable to see anything as new anymore. The feeling it gives me is being in the out-of-the-way places in the mountains where I went as a child. For us, too, there were those silent villages of old houses that seemed to grow out of the ground along with trees and shrubs, in the ancient confusion of things. However, this is *not* the first village we have seen, and everything refers back to first impressions. We find again the toothless lady, still bent over her tin like the other time, with a flowered skirt that comes to just below her knees, who knows how the skirt made its way up here. We again find the husband with a jacket in shreds, a sweater with holes, and a kind of dark skirt that could also be a pair of pants. Boubacar does his best so that they will recognize each of us, but I think that to them we are like the Chinese to European eyes, which is to say, all the same.

14 Tourists with their guides have arrived, coming along the ridge from the other direction. One is adorned with local necklaces and amulets, a ponytail. The American is reading tranquilly, as if he were in his own house, legs stretched out on a little table. The third is writing in his diary like me—who knows how many tourists come up here to write in their diaries. I'm listening to the evening chatter; Boubacar is talking about the tour guides. Under the preceding pro-Soviet government, everything was controlled by the Malian Society for the Development of Tourism, and private guides were arrested . . . the Dogon guides rebelled, etc. . . . . Now the other guide is talking about Italian cooperative organizations and the center in Bandiagara: "Cooperative robs the people . . . only the Germans . . ." The Center for Traditional Medicine doesn't do anything: "They give you medicine that never cures you . . ." Coppo is high profile, everyone knows him: "His center is a tourist monument, but the population doesn't benefit from it." They trail off into muttering. Jean is wandering around drinking from his water bottle, wearing his sunhat that looks like one a child would wear on a beach.

15 I took a shower in the latrine a little outside the village, three walls out in the open. As I was leaning against the wall, three big blocks came down and one part of the wall was destroyed. Relieving my bowels in that hole was impossible to consider . . . I have to note my initial reluctance as a tourist to talk with other tourists, who are, in contrast, all very friendly. A recap of those I've met: (1) a shaggy Italian, hair in a ponytail, a big thorax, who has traveled all of Africa, reads only books about Africa, has climbed many African mountains, arrived with a guide accompanied by (2) a skinny American who almost looks like Stan Laurel, who after his shower began to read a book of Faulkner short stories, speaks with a Midwestern accent, in the evening wears slippers, (3) a party of French-Belgians, with a young boy carrying their baggage, two men and three women, with whom we socialize before supper. They will sleep in the storeroom in the *case de passage*, we will sleep on the roof of the lady who is taking care of us, and Boubacar, I don't know where.

16 I was about to fall asleep, when Jean came back in the dark, climbing up the notched pole that serves as the stairs, and he wanted to talk to me. He had gone to watch evening Mass from outside the temple, which is Christian here, not that this changes much. The temple is outside the village, one hundred meters from the southern point of the oval, behind the *case de passage*. It is shaped like the old Dogon sanctuaries, with two buttresses on the sides, a narrow door in the middle, an undulating facade on the pediment. Inside, the Dogon temples are storage rooms of things that, to us, seem like trash, these being their old fetishes. (The masks are kept hidden in caves.) Jean says in the temple down there the only sacred image is a poster of Jesus Christ, with a candle in front of it. He was very moved by the people in kneeling position, by the religious functions carried on in the dark, the silence, the sacredness of other times. I'm writing by flashlight.

17 Slept on the roof, not even a buzzing in my ears, peacefully in a sleeping bag. I wake up in the night, the sky so dense with stars, truly *à la belle étoile,* searching for constellations I do not know. At five, the first women begin to leave the village with clothes to wash balanced on their heads, basins, buckets for getting water from the wells, walking on the paths of a big depression in the earth, not in groups, one at a time. Not a single voice from the village, complete silence, this is the country of silence. In the other direction, the men are leaving, heading toward the onion fields, if not there, then I don't know where they are going. They too walk singly, not in a group, silently, with hoes and calabashes, wearing those baggy trousers and sweaters, two or three of them wearing a jacket. Jean is sleeping, all twisted up and askew in his sleeping bag. You cannot see the sun yet, but all around are the yellow shadings of elucidation.

18 Breakfast together with the French-Belgian party, where, in reality, the youngest woman is Austrian and her German husband is from Munich. The Italian who reads only books on Africa is Roman, his name is Giovanni Cecchetti. The American (from Illinois?) tells me he is a great reader and asks if there are any interesting Italian authors translated in the United States. I cite Calvino, but he's never heard his name, and he recommends an American author unknown to me . . . We say good-byes before separating, all very friendly, smiles and handshakes (which is all very pleasant.) People encountered for one moment, maybe we will never see each other again, but when one is far away from his own territory, the defenses for protecting oneself from others fall away. On the ground, there is an empty can of preserves, which yesterday children were fighting over as if it were a toy. Boubacar hands over our empty mineral water bottles to the toothless lady, he says they will be used again. With him, you can't throw away anything, not even a piece of paper, he doesn't say a word, he just goes over to collect it. Children watching me write, piglets circulating, chickens pecking. Boubacar is in a hurry to leave, although we never see an urgent gesture coming from him, not even a trace of anxiety (this too being part of his art).

19 It took almost half a day to make the long trip down the Bandiagara Cliffs, where the vegetation becomes thick. We went down in order to then come up the other side, the side of the desert. I saw animals in the grass, I don't know what they were . . . A deserted depression, balanzan trees, baobabs, thorn bushes, birds. No one around except that man who stood up to yell, Boubacar acting the diplomat. Stopped in the shade of a baobab, I make the acquaintance of the minuscule knots of thorns, the *krem-krem*, which are incredibly annoying, inside my shoes. We talk as I'm pulling them out. Boubacar has discovered my age from Jean, and this changes everything because I too am an elder like the ones in the villages. Then, when he finds out that I write, an exclamation: "Finally, a writer!" Is he saying that he's met someone who lives by his art as he does? Something like that. From time to time he's philosophical, but you have to hold him down because he never gives an inch. And when I tell him that I would like it if he came to England so that I could take him walking in my places, he immediately stops me: "That's enough! Enough! I don't want to dream."

20 Evening. Stop for dinner and sleep at Kani-Kombolé (I think this is its name). Violet sky above the ridge, up there still a little light left and here, we're already in darkness. In the *case de passage* there are oil lamps, which give off limited light. The little girls wash dishes in a bucket nearly in the dark, the children play with something that's supposed to be a ball, but looks like a rag or a piece of tire. What comes back into my mind is the beauty of the onion fields we saw, incredibly green, with men stripped from the waist up, pouring water from the cal-abashes, and the heaps of stones along the path, a landscape of the Grand Canyon, gigantic blocks of sandstone strewn about, suspended from a small base, eroded from below by the wind and by now mountains balanced on the head of a pin, pinks that emerge out of creases in the rock as evening arrives, the man who greets me, the piglet, the chickens, the children, the toothless, smiling wife, drinking millet beer with Boubacar.

21 Morning. A break in the hike in the shade of a slab of sandstone. Boubacar's body is long, so lanky that it would be adolescent for us, even his face seems adolescent, his little mustache notwithstanding. He travels wearing gabardine pants, a dark sweater, backpack, Dogon cap, sunglasses, and, finally, that pair of patched-together shoes that are practically falling apart, the shoes with which he always picks the best path through the terrain. We don't speak with the people from here, we look at each other and smile. The most interaction we have had was last evening with the man who runs the *case de passage* after we were introduced by Boubacar. I thanked him for his welcome and he wished me well in life. This morning, his wife had a discrepancy in her accounts because two tourists had left without paying, and she thought that we had drunk the two bottles of mineral water. I offered to pay for them, but Boubacar didn't want me to. He says that they have to get used to the tourists. ("That will teach them.") We started up on our hike on a path full of prickly bushes; there are poisonous snakes in this area.

22 Evening, after the hike. I think the village is named Endé, but I don't want to ask, I'm resigned to not understanding much about these places. Seven o'clock. A cautious exploration of a little village lane, with sidelong glances, trying not to cross over the threshold of customs. At most, there are one hundred inhabitants here, maybe fewer, I would say. Narrow little lanes, two and a half or three meters, internal courtyards. The houses face each other and have similar facades, cubical shapes made of clay, flat roofs, cracked walls patched with mortar. In the evening they're dark, a few of them seem like checkered riverbeds due to the regularity of the concavities. Chickens, a piglet, a stone, nothing else in the alleyway. At this hour, everyone is inside a narrow family courtyard. Silence all around, the voice of a young girl somewhere, noises from tin pots. At this hour, at home, you hear televisions that explain what is happening in the world. I think of the journalist who asked me: "If you don't read newspapers, how do you keep in touch with the world?" What do they do here to keep in touch with the world? When I go back, I will have to say that I saw almost nothing of these villages, everything I do say I will have read in Griaule's book.

23 Toward Begnimato. When Boubacar walks you could track his footsteps with musical beats. A regular pacing adapted to the terrain, but also a lack of straining, the absence of acceleration, which gives the idea of moving in the current. On certain types of ground, this has the effect of regularizing the breathing of those who follow behind. I look at Jean's footsteps and they seem clumsy to me compared to Boubacar's cadence. Jean says that sometimes it looks like I'm going to collapse from exhaustion. I never ask myself where we are going. I think about the story of Cevenini and Ridolfi while the sky is covered with white clouds formed in regular streaks there up above the cliffs.

24 We're in a kind of scrubland, at the edge of the desert of sand. We're discussing how long it will take to loop around along the bottom of the Bandiagara Cliffs, to make the hard climb up, then to descend toward Bandiagara on the road to Dourou where the weekly market will be held in two days. (It's a five-day week here.) As we figure it, we won't be able to see the marvels of Banani, which is like the imperial Rome of Dogon country, clinging to the foot of the escarpment on perpendicular rock, with houses and granaries on all the crags of the gorge, plus those formations constructed like truncated cones which have such fantastic shapes (seen in a photo), and up above, the caverns of Tellem which exist truly in air. I also have the idea that Boubacar would not like going to those places because you enter the environs of Sanga where the government agencies control everything. He says it's more touristed there and that the inhabitants have learned to assault the *toubabs* in order to sell them their sculptures. According to him, the Dogon way of life is better preserved in this area. Well, in the final analysis, we're not going to see the Dogon Rome, but we will have crossed their countryside, as if we had gone to Calabria.

25 Sunset, 6:30. Walk along the foot of the cliffs harder than foreseen because of the sand. But the view across the desert of dunes makes up for the fatigue. The villages at the foot of the Bandiagara Cliffs, so near the sand dunes, are scattered about and not shaped in an oval, it seems to me. Or else they are offshoots of other villages, which are I don't know where. Asses greet us with braying. Little girls stare at us walking, then turn their heads away in order not to see us. Stripped baobab trees with regular cuts; the bark has many uses. The only village whose lanes we will pass through is Yawa, where we will meet the *hogon*, who must give us permission to go through so that we can then climb back up the cliffs. There are very few houses spread out underneath the cliffs, which are now in shadow. Boubacar, this evening, has gone to chat with the people who live here. Jean says we will sleep in the houses down there, with the asses, hoping they don't bray too much.

26 Morning in Yawa. Deserted village, except for those women who were threshing *fonio* and stopped doing so upon our arrival. Boubacar immediately made us turn our backs, I don't know why. The *hogon* lying on the ground, in a pathway two meters in size, leaning against the stairs of his sacred house, whose facade is different from the others but is no higher. He seemed half-asleep, with an arm resting on a step, wearing his dark Dogon clothing, but to my eyes he looked no different. Boubacar made a great display of respect in speaking to him, while the other did not lift his head. Then Jean handed him kola nuts, our ritual gift, and I don't remember whether we shook hands. We did not see one living soul in the surrounding small lanes. But up higher above, as we exited the village, an ancient woman stood up from behind a garden wall. Naked except for a skirt-cloth, skin like cracked leather, breasts like a deflated sack, a great protuberance shaped like a zucchini which came out from her stomach where the navel is. An old deaf-and-dumb woman, she had a great chat with Boubacar. Guttural sounds, gestures, and smiles, even for the two of us. Very contented and toothless, she grasped our hands, holding them between her palms, and it seemed as if she did not want to let us go.

27 On the ascent, I paid for every cigarette ever smoked during the course of my life. A climb up a rocky slope, a 20 percent rock-covered slope I would say, up under the wall of the cliff—even at that point I could hardly keep up my hiking pace. In order to get to the top, in addition to navigating the walkways that are like mule paths, the longitudinal faults, and climbing from rock to rock, the Dogon have built steps, logs forked at the top with notches for stairs. It's not a difficult climb, but it's a sheer drop below. Halfway up one of these stairways, the backpack twice as heavy, a buzzing of hornets started up that was so strong I couldn't hear or see anything else. A crisis of disorientation, of not knowing where I was, halfway up the steps, with a straight plummet below. From up above, Jean looked at me, worried, but he did not hear the buzzing in my ears. The imperturbable Boubacar reached down an arm for me, as if thinking about something else, pulled me up, and it was over thanks to his calmness. Right before this happened, I had noticed an old woman climbing up the same kind of ladder, only she had a bundle of sticks three times the size of my backpack, up there, slender and tranquil on the sheer face, she . . .

28 We are back, up on the high plain, a desert of dunes extending as far as the eye can see. A crossing over a lunar desert covered with white slabs, jumping from one to the other, and finally two small trees. We drink, stretched out on the ground, waiting to be able to resume our trek . . . Boubacar gave us a summary of all of Mali's empires and governments, from the great Songhai Empire to the coup against the pro-Soviet government, the popular revolt of 1992, and the coming to power of the current president. After which, he told us, quite clearly, that of all the guides, he is the most cultured because he reads books and the others do not. Another of Boubacar's observations: Dogon life is impenetrable because it is organized in water-tight compartments, and the secrets of one group are not known by another, taboos of one family are not those of another, the dialects are numerous and often not understood from one village to the next. This means that even he is a foreigner up here because only someone who grows up in the village knows the Dogon secrets. Yes, but he has his art, and, for example, right now, he knows exactly what time we will arrive in Dourou, even without a watch.

29 Evening in Dourou, our point of departure. We meet the French-Belgian-German group again. Sitting behind the outside wall of the *case de passage*, as we were eating rice and meat brought to us by the little girls, the three women of the group came looking for us. They wanted to chat after our meeting and finding the camaraderie that exists among enchanted tourists in a high-up village on the cliffs. For half an hour, lively, harmonious conversation, humorous banter, until the all-terrain vehicle arrived to carry away our visitors and their men. Good-byes, sadness at leaving us, exchanges of addresses, the departure of the all-terrain vehicle. At this point, a comment from Boubacar, impassive comic: "You can see how the three of us attract women, even though one of us is old" ("même avec l'âge"). He cannot quite fix my age within his parameters, because if I were from here, I would be one of the elders who gathered in the *case de palabre,* or even a *hogon* lying on the ground, doing nothing, from morning until night. We talk and laugh without thinking about the return trip. Buzzing in my ears, exhaustion, and quiet exaltation at being here. We sleep against the wall, Jean on a camping cot.

FIFTH NOTEBOOK

1 Began our return to Bandiagara in early afternoon, with something to write about in the album of textbook cases of African tourism. With the two rented mopeds that never stopped breaking down, backpacks forever falling, it was a half-comic adventure. Three times because of dirty spark plugs, six times from a punctured tire, in the middle of rocky ground and worn-out tires. Each time Boubacar left in search of a village to repair the tire, never tense, always unflappable, a slim pedaling figure with his Dogon cap. Each time we had a flat tire coming down from the high plain, there was a village nearby but we were unable to see it. Boubacar would leave, rolling the tire along the ground, and reappear a half hour later with tire inflated. That's how it went all afternoon until six in the evening, waiting for him along the side of the road, not being able to proceed with the other moped because immediately we would have become lost on the country lanes. We would sit there smoking, and each time someone would emerge from the millet fields to stare at us, then would go away. We wouldn't have seen a house or a living animal, but as soon as we sat down, someone would appear to look at us from a distance. The last time we had a flat tire, we were near a Bedouin kind of tent set up along the road, where two guys with a pot on the fire were making dinner. These two had a transistor radio that was playing music at the loudest volume, and the two of us were sitting there dismayed, but the ever-unflappable Boubacar announced: "A musical interlude."

2   After coming back from the high plain, it's as if we're in a daze, even more out of it than usual, in the suffocating bunker, with a john full of geckos. The documentary about the Dogon healers is never discussed anymore, which is just as well. But it's as if we have to put something back into motion, without knowing how to do it. It is like having to make a wheel start turning again, even though it is always the same wheel that starts turning again whenever it wants, and then we follow along out of inertia without giving it much thought. We found a note from Coppo apologizing to us for having been driven from his house. So therefore, all's well, niceness always cheers one up. We're in a bunker at the Center for Traditional Medicine, we'll try to take a shower.

3   Dined in Bandiagara, in the courtyard of a *buvette*. Four walls in the sand, serpentine alley getting here, a cockroach in the glass. This is the so-called ROTISSERIE MODERNE, with its name handwritten on a piece of wood. The owner: Ante Temely, who goes by Antonio, the antiquarian with the flashy smile, who at the baptism with the noble Ouoleghem talked to us in Spanish. Dined with Boubacar and one of his women friends. Boubacar had hooked us up again with the above-named Antonio, who went on about his passion for the flesh of ample women, the buttocks melting between the fingers, driving blue-eyed female tourists around on mopeds. Boubacar didn't approve of these discussions, but the two of them had already come to blows due to other disagreements, and they now keep at a safe distance. Boubacar considered Antonio's coarse discussions a lack of respect for me as the elder at the table. Antonio badmouthed the Center for Traditional Medicine, full of cassettes with taped interviews of Dogon healers, and it seems that a friend of his died from hemorrhoids, which were the result of transcribing these tapes for psychiatrists, sociologists, anthropologists. Antonio kept dwelling on the matter of the hemorrhoids, but this particular friend must have died as a result of being worn out from working "with the whites." Then Antonio took us to our dormitory in the savanna on his powerful Kawasaki motorcycle. Jean and I behind him on the seat, zigzagging at high speed in the dark and sand with his great belly laughs floating off in the wind.

4 Last day in Bandiagara. Now I would stay here for a long time, if I could, not however in the bunker for foreigners. With the last of the money: purchases that Jean wants to make at the market, plus the bus for Bamako. The day starts with breakfast in Antonio's *buvette*, Antonio, who is an art dealer, an interpreter/guide, descendant of the Dogon of Pelou, owner of the *buvette* and great seducer. He says he's not married, only engaged, but in the house of the *buvette* was his son who ran around naked. Antonio gave him huge spoonfuls of jam, getting his face all dirty. I did not see the mother. Instead, our Antonio has created for himself the bedroom of a seducer behind the antiquarian shop, with posters of rock singers hung up, some pictures of women with large breasts. Upon returning to England, I'm supposed to call an English girl named Suzannah, saying that he, Antonio di Bandiagara, always thinks about her blue eyes . . .

5 Trip to the market with Jean and Boubacar. Jean wanted to buy some indigo clothing, relying on bargaining in the local language of our guide. Instead, he discovered that Boubacar doesn't like to haggle over prices with the vendors because he says that it's not his style. At the market, I was drawn to everything, and I was stirred by unexpected pangs of emotion at the mere sight of a mound of old tires. I would have liked to meet that lady who comes from the Ivory Coast and speaks magnificent French, or else to stop a while to chat with others, with whoever was there at the market. But Boubacar did not have time, he came only because Jean had asked him to, he made no secret of it. He is the type who gets straight to the point, a blasé urbanite of the savanna . . . Then we fell into the hands of Antonio, who made us eat in his *buvette*. He talked to us about everything, with great outbursts of laughter which no one paid any attention to, he gave us advice about the return trip to Bamako, he took us for a ride on his motorcycle, and he succeeded in selling us some Dogon footstools and some varied amulets for our last few pennies. Tomorrow morning he will come to get us with his motorcycle.

6 The one who goes by the name of Alì, who the other day helped us with the moped coming back from the high plain, came looking for us at night in our bunker, bringing with him a friend who sells statuettes. We shook hands, I sent him off. A half hour later they came back in the dark to try selling us the same items; Jean was already sleeping. I again politely sent away the antiquarian. "Tomorrow?" "We don't have any more money." Last night an all-terrain vehicle arrived with three anthropologists, who are now already heading back to the savanna. The wind shakes the trees in front of the domes of the guest quarters. Jean sleeps, the john is invaded by geckos, the crows are cawing, caw, caw.

7 Everything in a hurry. Antonio was busy with bus tickets, we entrusted him with our money. Then we discovered that the manager of the preselected bus was his brother. The one assigned to baggage insisted that we pay an additional fee for the backpacks, treating us in a truly ugly way, like two cows to be milked. I went to tell Antonio's brother: "Wait a minute here!" The Temely brother came over to give the porter what for—he would not stand for it again! . . . Everyone was at the departure. The aristocratic Amadou Ouoleghem came to say good-bye to us, on a bicycle. He was sorry to have chatted so little with us; he said he hoped that we would see each other again in the future. The three boys were there as well, Samou, Abou, Boubou, whom we had neglected too much. Antonio shooed away the children who were trying to get close to us, he stood planted there like a guard, with his dark tourist sunglasses, the Fiorucci brand. Our friend Amadou was not there, who moves only to go shopping, and otherwise remains enclosed within the walls of that garden in permanence. Kind Amadou: Amadou the Permanent.

8 Eight hundred kilometers to cover in the bus, with a departure time of four o'clock, arrival tomorrow morning in Bamako. More crammed together than the bus we arrived on. Uncomfortable to sit, there's no place to put your legs. Stops at sunset for prayers. The bending of heads in the sand, hands raised up toward God, nothing overly devout in those praying, everything so tranquil that a desire to pray with them comes over me. Leave again at dusk. Frightening jolts because of the potholes, constant detours, but Jean notes that the babies never cry. There are many attached to mothers, but they never cry. The savanna disappears in the dark and I try to sleep with this narrow slot for my legs . . . The policeman comes to mind, the one who was thin, small, with a thin mustache, cap worn at a jaunty angle, very self-important in his role, who talked to me at the roadblock in Sévaré. He asked me, "Doctor?" "No, I write." "A writer?" "Yes." "So then you're a doctor of words!" Then I remember the approval in his face, nodding his head, when what slipped out of my mouth was "Love at first sight" (with regard to Mali). He had about him the air of a refined expert on rhetoric.

9 At a standstill again, before Ségou, 3:30 in the middle of the night, in front of that same shop where we stopped on the way going. The vendors selling drinks, pieces of mutton in a bowl, various kinds of canned food, everyone seated with their banquets spread out before them waiting, with lanterns. Some kids were playing, making a tremendous hubbub, closing up a playmate in a container that serves as an icebox, in stitches over the joke. Jean, wandering around, keeping to himself, was drinking Coca-Cola and eating peanuts. I can still remember the little square in front of the shop near Ségou, it was a calm, aimless night. And now, this now, empty moment that changes with a staggering quickness. The sun is coming up, we pass by the lights of the villages. Each moment goes away on its own, the curtain opens, I perform my recitation, then I don't have time to continue it because it's necessary to move on. It is like a game of leaving, always leaving, going through the door a little surreptitiously, blending oneself with the shadows. Noise of the wind: whoosh!

10 Another stop, now in the first light of dawn. Everyone on the bus has to pee, I don't know according to which synchronism. Men and women over by the bushes twenty meters away, everyone bent down, no one hiding himself, lined up there peeing. We are standing next to the bus watching the show, we whites, always out of place . . . Boubacar did not come to say good-bye to us at the departure because he had that woman friend he's concerned about, but also because he is a person with a lot to do, a tourist guide with his name in the famous *Lonely Planet*. However, we have the impression that he was very happy talking to us about his art and teasing us to keep us in good spirits. He had proposed that we exchange clothes or something else, in order to have something he lacks and can't buy for himself, for example, shoes, which he is in dire need of. At our last dinner, when I sprung the idea that Jean should make a documentary on his work as a guide who goes through the Dogon villages, but most of all about his art as a walker, Boubacar said: "Don't talk to me about things that will make me dream." "But when you're just talking one always dreams a little." "Okay, tonight, I'll be open-minded."

11 Around seven, mounds of trash lining the sides of the street for two or three kilometers. Dust everywhere, streets in a mess, a succession of shanties and mud where people are lighting a fire. We arrive in a clamorous chaos of buses and taxis at the station where the buses for Sogoniko depart. Jean says that we are Cevenini and Ridolfi . . . Complete exhaustion. When I go to the bathroom, feces reddened by the sand, clothes completely red and covered with sand. Now Bamako seems to me like a familiar place, a grace-given refuge, like a free port to which we are returning.

12 Pool in the morning, Hôtel de l'Amitié, into which we have relapsed due to inertia. I ate too much at breakfast, looking at the other hotel guests who in the morning wolf down croissants, bread and butter, guava jam, mango jam, bacon, eggs, cantaloupe, watermelon, canned fruit, oat flakes, yogurt, steaks. I recall an illness called *latah* by Malians: if a person is *latah* and sees someone make a gesture or even sees branches moving in the wind, he imitates that gesture or that movement of the branches without being able to stop anymore. In the Hôtel de l'Amitié one lives under a *latah* spell.

13 Cloudy sky, without a breath of wind, it's suffocating. Around eight o'clock, there's no one poolside, the tourists are still sleeping. There are only the attendants who are sweeping and arranging the lounge chairs. Yesterday we slept nearly all day long . . . Nighttime things. Dream in different languages where someone said to me: "Dr. Schmerz's treatment . . . it tooth le désespoir mal placé." I woke up deciphering this strange phrase, with the memory of a science-fiction panorama where all languages were mixed together. It seems to me that "tooth" stands for the French *tue,* kill, but having something to do with teeth. As far as Dr. Schmerz, he was my white healer substituted for the Dogon ones, and I imagine him with big teeth.

14 I'm looking at the little Dogon wooden granary door that I bought in a village on the high plain. There are three rabbit heads carved in (the totemic animal), then the *hogon's* house (the linchpin of every village) and two heads that no one has been able to identify (perhaps the original couple?). Everything in these carvings makes me think of masks, a thought that speaks through masks. For those people, all the secrets of the world are contained in masks, because masks are the dead who are reincarnated into the living. And our naked face for them says nothing perhaps . . . Here, now, tallying up our trip among the Dogon, I would have to say that I saw little and understood even less. But I have an absurd nostalgia for those places, and Jean does too.

15 Jean studies the trip to Senegal on the Bamako-Dakar train. According to Ariane's phone call, it's a sure thing that Jean's documentary would fit into Thomas Harlan's project. But which documentary? Then I find out that, what's more, Thomas is suggesting starting it on the Dakar-Bamako train, with the idea of stopping in the savanna with his troupe of actors, to perform a part of Shakespeare's *Tempest*. It's necessary to find out if that train will be suitable for the shooting. But shooting what? . . . Today we saw our friend Ibrahim again, who was sick with malaria, has lost a lot of weight, also because during Ramadan he couldn't eat during the day. So emaciated, in the newspaper shop of the hotel's hallway, I had not even recognized him. He's always tired, always looking for a place to sit down.

16 For our textbook cases of African tourism, Jean suggests recording the one from today with the four Canadians in search of gold. Actually, they were invited by a Canadian company that works Malian gold mines, because Mali does not have the means to exploit them itself. There are four from Quebec, three men and one woman, who had already drunk a case of liter-sized beers. They invited us to drink, the first whites in this hotel who don't run away from other whites, I should add. But the conversation was a disaster, because the gangly one blabbered on a mile a minute, completely smashed. This guy, bare chest, baseball cap, hair like a hippy, short shorts, heavy military boots, was in the grips of a hebephrenic fixation. This is how he had his fun: calling over the hotel's vendors, those selling statuettes and jewelry, that is to say, calling them and saying he wanted to buy a Tuareg sword. Happily, they hurried to poolside. Something like this had never happened, someone calling them over to buy their merchandise, it's always them running after the hotel's customers with a certain perseverance. At this point, the gold hunter started to wave around a wad of dollar bills to really get their attention, saying he was a connoisseur and his house in Quebec was full of African artifacts. Then he examined the Tuareg sword and said it was flawed, that he knew about these things. He found defects in everything they brought him, so that he offered a ridiculously low sum for the whole lot of African artifacts, waving around his wad of dollars. The local vendors went crazy, not being able to follow this kind of talk coming from a drunk with dollars, with his Quebec French. After a while, they were offended by the figure offered, which was a true insult to their trade as dealers. But he ranted and raved, always going back to talking about the technical defects of the Tuareg sword, which according to him was rusting in the hilt, I don't know why. So the dealers, one by one, went away offended by undignified behavior. But right away after, the drunk, waving his baseball cap, sent the pool boy to call them back. They returned, ever so quietly, the same figure was repeated, etc. In the evening, in the hall, he had spread terror. All the vendors hid around corners, he had discombobulated them. But he went around waving a twenty-dollar bill, yelling loudly that he had finally decided to buy a Tuareg dagger: "Venez, venez!" The vendors went out of their minds, hoping for a miracle. They even sent emissaries to scout it out, among them a beautiful young lady with a veil embroidered with gold. So then the gangly one wanted to have the young lady try on all the necklaces displayed in the hall, without ever deciding, because they were all defective, according to him. The others anxiously spied from around the corners. With his delusions as a drunken gold hunter he had brought an uncharacteristic animation into the hall, waving his baseball cap and extremely pleased to have put on a show. But the tourists pretended to be unaware of him, quickly slipping into the elevators.

17 At least I'm able to write well in this Hôtel de l'Amitié, by the side of the pool in the morning or afternoon, because the place inspires the observations of a spectator behind a window. Another example of African tourism to record, minor but almost moving. I met two Italian tourists in the elevator: one small, petulant, a wife who's always blaming her husband; a mild-mannered husband whom she makes miserable and who acknowledges his faults, above all when his wife is nervous. In the elevator they did not look at me, because they were talking about what to do during the next two hours, as if it were a question of life and death. Now they're not doing anything and they are lying in the sun not far from me at the side of the pool. They do not speak to each other, she lies with her back naked, he leafs through an Italian newspaper. The only thing said was what popped into the husband's mind a little bit ago, and it was this: "Did you know that Bucci got a vacation on the company because he had sold so much?" The wife did not reply. The husband looked in the other direction, depressed, sighing.

18 This afternoon, visit to the Mali Center for Cinematography. It is at the rear of one of those courtyards of various government offices. A plaque at the entrance says, UNIVERSITÀ DEL MALI, and underneath, ISTITUTO DELLE BELLE ARTI. The institute of fine arts is a big shed made of masonry with a sandy open space in front, where there were men sitting on the ground busy making objects of art. Some of them were cutting iron, others were working on statuettes like those on sale to tourists. We came to a little gray office building at the rear of the courtyard, and immediately inside there was a man in the hallway praying on a small prayer rug. We went up the stairs, came back down the stairs. We couldn't find the right office because everything was marked with incomprehensible governmental acronyms. So, confused by the acronym we were looking for, we were welcomed, with great politeness, into the office of the man who had just been praying. Jean explained about the project of making a documentary in Mali, he wanted some information to pass along to Thomas Harlan. The man said immediately that he too was in the film industry and he treated Jean as a colleague. Then he related how there were troupes from all over the world who came here to film location shots or advertising clips, especially in the desert near Timbuktu. The government supervised the film troupes upon their arrival, so it was therefore necessary to present a project that would be evaluated, to put up a security deposit, and, from the moment shooting begins, to retain a government guide who is paid so much each day. I was amazed by the inexhaustible courtesy of the man in responding to Jean's questions, adding news about people in the Malian film industry. All the solemnity of government offices had the flavor of dreams in which you don't know what's going on anymore, but you can't move because of weariness. That was us, in a cinematographic dream without beginning or end, we listened to the man who told us about the advertising clips he had directed and about the fact that tomorrow he would be going to Gao to film another one. From behind the bureaucrat's table, he treated us like guests in his home, and at the end, handshakes, nothing settled. We found ourselves back on the street like two idlers who were trying to make evening come sooner. The birds in the trees behind the hotel made an unbearable racket.

19 Day by the side of the pool doing nothing, aside from scribbling about Cevenini and Ridolfi, but still in a state of *latah*. In the elevator, the guests are put out by having to respond to a greeting, so as a result each encounter becomes annoying. Assaults by little kids on the street, but if you walk straight ahead, without batting an eyelash when they call you, you disarm them with this surprise move. Yesterday evening, by now reckless spendthrifts, we went out to eat at the restaurant Djenné. The girl who served us: an elegance turned Cevenini and Ridolfi's heads every thirty seconds, even if she wore the usual clothing, a kind of uniform, turban, tunic, and a skirt-cloth tied around her waist that was not very colorful. The absolute resides within that which is nothing special at all, which is absolutely necessitated (Ridolfi's idea, Spinozist).

20 Evening, in our room. I'm recording another textbook example of African tourism, for people who read *Le Monde Diplomatique*. Today Ibrahim took us to visit the village of Boukoro, an hour from Bamako by car. Jean had read in *Le Monde Diplomatique* that the Canadian cooperative organization has helped people of that village create new kinds of culture, and in this way the village would become rich. We left very curious about seeing how a rich village looked, in Mali . . . It was a village built along a street like many others. We asked where the new cultivations were located, that is to say Ibrahim asked and then he guided us there on foot. This trek began among the stubble in the millet fields, through narrow paths, past bushes and dips in the ground, then through a mango grove. There at the end, there were old farms, huts, but not even a hint of big cultivation projects. Maybe we had the wrong village? Ibrahim asked about it. Nearby, there were a few gardens, like the communal plots granted to elderly people in Italy. Tiny fenced-in gardens of green vegetables, legumes, tomatoes. These were the new types of culture they were talking about in *Le Monde Diplomatique* . . . Going back near the main road, we found a kind of gazebo built in the local style, with three young Canadians who offered us ginger juice and good conversation. The girl sociologist explained to us everything about the cooperation between the village of Boukoro and the village of St. Elisabeth in Quebec. She said that the residents of St. Elisabeth applied for a loan on behalf of the savanna dwellers of Boukoro for the acquisition of seeds, so that these people could grow vegetables for their meals (*le piment,* as they say here), instead of having to buy them at the market. That was it, nothing new in the way of cultivation. Then someone from the village arrived, the propagandistic-politician type, with a bag, a beret, and pamphlets about the Canadian cooperative organization. It was he who had given the information to *Le Monde Diplomatique*, making it into an example of new African economic development. He thought that we wanted to interview him, too, and I think he was disappointed when he found out we weren't journalists. He even asked Ibrahim if he wanted to interview him.

21 On the streets of Bamako there are these wooden booths in the form of a pyramid, where one buys tickets for the *tiercé*, the horse racing lottery. Today, Ibrahim's confession about the fact that he always ends up at the lottery booth, repeating to himself, "I'm not playing, I'm not playing, I must not play, the only way to win is to not play." Then, every time he falls for it and bets the little bit of money he has. The car he drives is not his, but belongs to the ancient head of the Traoré family, and Ibrahim has to pay him something for the use of it: "If I could just save a little money . . ." But this situation with the *tiercé* eats up all of his budget. What would he do, if he won? Buy things for the family, he says, in addition to buying himself a camera which he really wants: yes, but most of all so he could photograph family festivities (the rest of the world holds little attraction for him) . . . Jean, preoccupied, broods over the documentary project. He doesn't know anymore what it should be, given that, according to Thomas Harlan, it should begin on the Dakar-Bamako train, the legendary train, and he has to study the possibility of filming. I don't know what to say, the story about Cevenini and Ridolfi goes forward.

22 This morning went to the train station to get tickets for the Bamako-Dakar trip. Remembering the station, the chaos of vendors, the wait for tickets, the prostitute in the waiting room, the civil servant's cubbyhole, and our unusual situation, rare whites who want to take the Bamako-Dakar train, where during the night robbers lower themselves from the roof of the cars into the windows and steal everything, they say. Coming back, on the street, we ran into the Italian we had met on the Dogon high plain, the one who reads books only about Africa,

Giovanni Cecchetti, who was about to leave on a pirogue for Koulikoro. But today is really the day for meeting people again, for surprise encounters. In the evening in the restaurant near the Niger, a huge room painted in an acidic green, idle waiters, running into Françoise Mairey whom I had not seen for fifteen years. In Bamako! Together with a new husband, a very thin Malian from a village near Kayes. My head spinning, a fragment remains of Paris fifteen years ago, it wasn't really a welcome encounter. Today I don't want to see Françoise again, because I don't want to talk about the past, memories, stories, etc.—here there is only the blessed present, the horizon line of events, the rest is a dust cloud of phantoms.

23 In late morning, and until afternoon, a loudspeaker from the nearby mosque transmitted the voice of a religious figure, I don't know who he is. An enraged, bitter voice, which smacked of Holy War, hearkening to a Koran of Vendetta, sending it out into the air for four hours. We could hardly talk to one another because of the constant screaming, in the name of Allah, that hit the ears. I asked Ibrahim what he was saying and Ibrahim, who was very calm, explained: "He is talking about what is good and what is evil." That voice gave the impression of waiting for the Final Judgment, Jean says, with the threat of having to suffer the pains of hell if one does not behave correctly. In Europe there is no need for all this hullabaloo on Good and Evil: for us that threat creeps up on you silently from behind, when you begin to feel loneliness, with the absence of replies outside the general consensus, and you become like a telephone for which the bill must be paid, but which is officially considered inoperable, insofar as you have become "outmoded." Chatting before dinner, with the desert wind that brings a suffocating heat, the harmattan.

24 At dinner in the restaurant of the Hôtel de l'Amitié. When we arrived there was no one except a very pompous, corpulent black man in a loose-fitting boubou which he continually

rolled up on his shoulders, a briefcase on the floor. In front of
him he had a great variety of plates and he ate with relish, alone
in the dining room. As we went to sit down at the table next to
his, I said hello to him. By way of response he looked me up and
down, but instead of uttering words he made a resonant sucking
sound between his molars, as if to tell me that he was eating and
did not want to say hello to us. After which, eating, he made
every possible noise with his mouth, small belches, palatal
sounds of satisfaction, guttural sounds to clear his throat, gulps
in order to swallow better, satisfied exhalations drinking his
Fanta. All of these sounds admirably expressed the idea that we
should not disturb him, intent as he was on his digestion, besides
being an important police officer. This much we understood
when the maître d' came over and engaged him in dutiful conversation. The other one made his replies without looking up
from his plate. I would never have hoped to meet a high-ranking
police officer face to face, and one so extraordinarily fitting with
my fantasies about government and police officials here. (A
functionary from one of those offices that you see at the rear of
courtyards, colonial type, with big signs in colonial French
above the door.) Such a person epitomizes absolute and indis-
putable law, right in front of two haggard tourists who must listen to him and feel very humble. This man made this perfectly
clear to us when he stood up to leave and, brushing against our
table, let out an impressive belch.

25 During these days in Bamako, at the end of each afternoon, I wait for the moment to take an evening stroll
around the streets of the Medina. On the great two-laned boulevard, the Route de Koulikoro, at the hour the neon rods light up
everywhere above the doors, people sit on steps, in air that is
filled with dust. Nobody is selling anything anymore, the stalls
are closed up with rope. It's a party because the day is over, and
wherever you look everyone is there chatting. Not one single
person who passes by is in a hurry. It's the same on the street as
it is on the sidewalk because cars no longer have the right of way

over pedestrians. A few shop doors are open, and you see merchants who are playing dominoes. One understands the hour by people's movements, always more relaxed toward evening. The impression is one of being in the country in the evening, in summer, but in a countryside full of houses. Someone carries on a conversation in the shade, a girl goes to get water from the pump again, someone a little ways off plays the conjurer from the bush, some fat ladies fan themselves in front of a house, some thin men pick their teeth. Someone sleeps on the ground. A young lady in hot pants goes to work in search of males. Bands of kids run behind some tourist, and in the doorway of the restaurant Djenné, one sees that doorman dressed like Lothar in the old comic strip . . . On returning from the stroll this evening, Ibrahim was sad because we had not yet given him our addresses. He had wanted us to go to dinner at his house, one night, his mother was going to prepare us a *tiédoudienne* ("but free of charge"). Leave-taking is complex, it's hard to find words to say. Jean was a little shaken up, looking away. I told Ibrahim to stop playing the *tiercé*. But for the first time he seemed absent to us, besides being too thin and worn out by the after-effects of malaria. It seemed as if we had betrayed him, not warning him in time about our departure.

SIXTH NOTEBOOK

1 Morning, nine o'clock. We're on the Bamako-Dakar train, already settled into the sleeping car. In the square between the tracks, which is red from dust, people hang around waiting, many rubbing their teeth with the little stick. Vendors of rugs, of electric flashlights, of bread. Lots of hustle and bustle, but nearly everyone with the little stick toothbrush, a few actually with a twig that still has leaves. In the middle of the tracks, one of them wanders selling raincoats, very demure, wearing one raincoat, one on his shoulder, a third on a crutch. Beneath us, a man and two young women are saying good-bye, the women embracing each other and touching each other's hair, one of the two women is departing. In fact, now she's come up right into our compartment. Introductions, we'll be traveling companions in the sleeping car . . . We had thought that this would be a special African-style train, in light of Thomas Harlan's documentary and plans. Instead, it's like a slow Milan-Bari train. We don't really know how long the trip will take because there are a lot of rumors circulating. The young woman in our compartment says that it was forty-eight hours late coming from Dakar. Even the number of stops is incredibly high, but varies according to the rumor.

2 First stop. Our companion in the compartment is named Sarr Batouly, works as a secretary in Dakar, was on vacation for a month in Bamako visiting a friend. She is plagued by the watchman for the sleeping cars, who comes in to whisper propositions to her and tries to touch her. She responds by laughing as if it's a joke, but he really does feel her up and down. Now he brings her a transistor radio, and in giving it to her touches her some more, then he takes away the transistor, laughing. They speak in Wolof. He is the kind who is amiably crude, in a grease-stained tee shirt . . . From the compartment, in front of us, we see a high plain. There is another track with a train loaded with wood, and on the other side, a village of hovels made of clay. Vendors selling everything climb up from the slope before the village, but in particular it is women and children who are selling food. Their cries are a song, three-note modulations. Onions, sweet potatoes, eggplants, bananas, yellow oranges. Jean is talking with someone in the aisle. He'll readily talk your ear off, he's like Cevenini.

3 Morning, 11:30. Now we are passing through a valley completely covered with garbage bags. The persecution by the watchman of the sleeping car continues, and he comes by with another watchman to visit our Sarr Batouly. She speaks only with her eyes, and besides that she tries to fend off the watchman's hands, but always laughing. Monotonous crossing of the bush, whitish sky. Jean calculates the number of stops, telling me names that I don't understand . . . The savanna always the same. Villages of circular huts, scattered throughout in the scrubland. It seems that we're at Sibikoro, small village encircled by a wall. Cylindrical huts with truncated cone roofs, covered with faggots or millet canes. Blinding heat on the train and savanna.

4 The sleeping car watchman has come to sleep in the empty berth, up above, but dangles an arm in order to touch our Sarr Batouly even as she sleeps. Now the train track passes right through the middle of a village, with walls, narrow streets on either side. This one must really be more populated than the others because the assault on the train by the vendors is more massive. Truly a throng. Hands thrust toward the windows offer bananas, oranges, a kind of corn, other things, with that modulated three-note cry plus a stop-beat. A village every fifteen or twenty minutes, you realize that it exists when you see a path in the unpopulated savanna, and if there's a path, then comes a village.

5 Early afternoon. Stop at Boukouto, village with old colonial agricultural settlements which I see in the background, and it seems to me we're close to Codigoro in Italy. A visit to the food car. People pray on a rug in the aisle and they have to move when we pass by. The restaurant is the only part of the train that would be good for filming. Long hall with decorations that are slightly primitive, deafening noise, it seems like a colonial tavern. As for the rest, hard to film in the narrow and crowded aisles. And as for Thomas Harlan's idea of stopping in a village to perform Shakespeare's *Tempest,* I try to imagine what the savanna-dwellers would say about it . . . The watchman for the sleeping car has woken up, he bums one cigarette after another from me, an incredibly fast smoker. When he leaves, I study this Sarr Batouly, who studies me as I write, and I discover that I like her. She is shortish and a little plump beneath the blue jacket, an impenetrable face because it passes from a laugh to a scowl, with nothing in between . . . A Frenchman talks with Jean in the aisle and says that in Kayes the police try to make you pay for stamping your passport. We needed to declare in Bamako that we were exiting Mali, now there's the risk that they'll withhold our passports to squeeze some money out of us.

6 Jean is starting to think that even this documentary on the train is not feasible. I say that the savanna is a great spectacle, he says it's monotonous. We're stopped at Bangala, small group of huts in the savanna. A mutual aid bond has been established with Sarr Batouly, and we exchange cigarettes, cookies, vitamins, sleeping pills. Now the savanna is fairly green, there is no more of that land consisting of red sand like this morning. The green of the trees is mixed with the yellow of the grasses. In truth, the vegetation is sparse, scattered trees, few bushes, sand paths. The sky has taken on a color between deep blue and a pale ash-gray. How long will the trip last? Sarr Batouly, in a blue jacket decorated with gold thread, has gone to sleep in the sleeping car, with her back turned. It's too hot, and I'm trying to sleep, too.

7 I wake up again, six o'clock. At times the savanna seems like a steppe. Now it's like a sick forest, where the little plants have become thin, the grass dried out, and only a few trees are able to rise up with their green foliage; there's a contrast between these giants with green foliage and the gray bushes all around. Other times, you see large black blotches, where the savanna is burned, trees burned to ashes, bushes blackened with smoke . . . The Frenchman who has struck up a friendship with Jean is traveling by motorcycle, which is now loaded onto the train. He too is a textbook case of African tourism, but of the more adventurous type from the olden days. He comes from Bordeaux, by motorcycle, and he has crossed Algeria and Mauritania alone. He went from Dakar to Bamako by motorcycle, following narrow dirt paths, sleeping in the villages on the savanna, not worried about malaria and parasites. He's in a car without a sleeping berth together with Senegalese, where a little while ago he ate with the others from the same plate, he laughed and licked his fingers with pleasure.

8 We arrive in a big village that maybe is called Mailà (these names that I write down are always very uncertain). Afterwards, we pass a river two times larger than the Po. On the banks women are bathing, soaping themselves from head to toe. On the other side of the bridge there is a real town, with many houses made of masonry and gas stations, an ass that is grazing in the middle of the piazza, an old man with the white *cecià* seated under the TOTAL sign. The market, traffic of vendors, children with buckets of water, women covered with colorful shawls. I keep writing my notes, sitting on the edge of the sleeping car bed, and my companion in the opposite compartment very intently observes me writing, her eyes staring, sometimes for as long as five minutes.

9 Sarr Batouly is worried about us because of the business with the passport stamps. She says that the police commissioner from Kayes is traveling in the next car, and he can give me an explanation. While this commissioner is at the window, I go to ask him if it's necessary to declare our exiting Mali in Bamako. He replies rigidly, in bureaucratic French. He says that the officials at the border will do what they have to do, there's no problem. I don't understand a thing. The explanation done, I humbly thank him. He goes back into his compartment to talk with his wife, he has taken care of official business. It reminds me of an expression that my father used to use for those types, he said that they were full of themselves.

10 Now the savanna is a big yellow grassland, the sun is going down, reddish reflections in the train. There is a dirt path, thirty centimeters wide, that runs along the track. The Frenchman from Bordeaux has traveled on motorcycle paths like this, day after day, and he was content . . . It is eight at night. After rocky and hilly countryside, the train is stopped for a half hour in a gully. Great palms wave on a ridge. We're already late, says a very fat and very black gentleman who has emerged from the fourth berth. I ask myself, late for what, I'm just fine here.

11 About ten at night, we're getting close to Kayes. The police commissioner's wife talks in the aisle with a police official. She always replies with silly giggling, making movements with her hips as well in a beautiful traditional dress that wraps around her. One could say that she is right from the mold of the wife of a police commissioner who is full of himself. But what is a police commissioner's wife, a mold that's a given? Maybe we're all born like this, already fixed types with one destiny. One is already a commissioner's wife from the cradle, one already a prefect, one already principal . . . Her giggling continues in the aisle, and I don't understand what it means because the official is speaking to her in a very serious tone. But also very insistent, he doesn't ever stop the discourse, sometimes lowering his voice. As in an old Russian novel where there's an official who's playing the gallant with the prefect's wife: respectful and tantalizing remarks, made in a soft voice, and she laughs so she doesn't have to answer yes or no.

12 At Kayes, the moon has come up above the high plain and it is a full moon. We are stopped for half an hour; a good many of the cars have emptied, people are camped out on the sidewalk to eat. I'm waiting for Jean, who, together with the Frenchman from Bordeaux, has gone to have the passports stamped. So as a result, I'm here without a passport or ticket, a little lost in the night like Ridolfi, under the protection of this Sarr Batouly, whom all the males come to court, taking turns, in an almost nonstop line. However, she still pays a lot of attention to me, I am still writing, she considers me a very peculiar guy, maybe a little maniacal . . . Big station with many trains carrying freight, there in the rear, some lights. A freight car is in motion, some men jump on it quickly, each with a little bundle of rags on his back. In the dim background, large houses lit up by that neon tube, and the moon . . .

13 Morning. Near Tambacounda. Anxious night until six. At Kayes, last station before the Senegal border, the police said they couldn't find the stamp necessary to put the exit visa on our passports. There in their office, they opened drawers and said: "It's not there." They kept our passports, sending Jean and the Frenchman back onto the train: "*We'll* bring them to you." The Frenchman had found himself in a situation like this before, and he said that it's a trick to get us to fork over money. "The Mali police, 99 percent corrupt," he said, repeating this statistic. We waited in the car, fearing that the train would depart before they brought us our passports. Also because it wasn't clear how long the train stop would be; it had already lasted five hours. Someone said that it was because of the candles. But which candles? Sarr Batouly was interested in our situation, truly worried for us. Discussions with other travelers who came to court her . . . At a certain point I got down off the train in search of the police office and I immediately got lost in the throng. On top of it, anxious Jean wanted me to go back to the compartment, afraid that they would steal our baggage. "How? Our Sarr Batouly is there." He ignored what I was saying. Back and forth between our compartment and the Frenchman's. I was agitated, no longer enchanted, waiting for the arrival of the police who wanted to squeeze some money out of us. But the Frenchman's friendliness with the Senegalese had yielded benefits, insofar as the Senegalese train guard is in his compartment, and he went to get our stamped passports. Small, skinny, an intense and self-assured type, in green uniform, he went to the Mali police and told them off. Came back calmly, gentlemanly, with the passports, right before departure. This, around four . . .

At five, stop at Koroko, the first station on the other side of the border. An imposing Senegalese official enters the compartment, orders me to follow him with our passports (mine and Jean's.) Making my way in the dark running behind him, passing through a freight car packed with sleeping bodies. An American and a white woman whom the official called "the German" ran behind me. We came to the large square in front of the police station, with only the weak light of a wall lamp, and about a hundred people assaulting a table where they were supposed to register identity cards. (At that time of night? Unbelievable!) One soldier seated at the table registered names in a thick colonial-type book, while an infinite number of arms stretched out to hand him documents. The white woman called the German was behind me with a worried look in that mass of blacks. It was necessary to declare one's line of work in a loud voice. The soldier wrote it down in the thick book, just that. Who knows why he was interested in my line of work? On the way back, we whites introduced ourselves in the dark. The young American man was an agricultural technician, in Mali already for a year. The other was an Englishwoman (sociologist?) in camouflage explorer's pants, who at my first quip shut me down with an icy stare. Then, in the compartment, another long wait with mosquitoes buzzing, and finally a short sleep came.

14 Ten-thirty. We woke up at nine, the entire train in the best possible mood. Now, however, we have decided to get off it because we don't know exactly when it will arrive in Dakar. Theories circulating fluctuate remarkably, anywhere between this evening and tomorrow afternoon. Sarr Batouly is making a face because we are abandoning her to suitors ("They're bothering me"), and she extracts a promise that we will call her in Dakar. She asks Jean if I wrote all night long while she was sleeping, perhaps a little worried about this mania of mine. She complains to me that all the wooing has been too much, saying that with us she feels like she's among family.

15 Tambacounda. The railroad yard is a confusion of carts pulled by asses, porters of every race, children who sell cigarettes. Since this morning Jean has assumed the role of leader, and now he has gone to get information about the bush taxi. The abandoning of the train was chaotic because there was the assault by male and female vendors, soldiers who were getting off, the sidewalk thick with baggage and boxes and crates. Running along, we almost lost each other, then found ourselves here in this piazza. Jean's coming back . . .

16 Village outside Tamba. When the children attacked us in force at the bus station, I did not obey my leader's orders, and so we found ourselves in a situation in which one group of assailants wanted to load us onto a bus for Dakar and another onto a bus for the Casamance region. Now, the Casamance was precisely where I wanted to go, while Jean wanted to go to Dakar. However, then someone said that in the Casamance there is unrest, it is dangerous to wander around the countryside, and that I would do better to go to Dakar as well. This produced the rejoining of forces, with a battle to take me away from those who wanted to put me on the bus to the Casamance. In the confusion, everyone pulled us this way and that, the reason why at a certain point Jean was about to go by himself to the Casamance, and me, to Dakar where I had no reason to be. But a wise old man who was selling leaflets from the Koran understood that there had been a mistake, and stopped the action by blowing a whistle. Then, with minimal gesturing he sent off our assailants, and we followed him through a narrow street in the direction of the open savanna without understanding where he was taking us. However, I thought he was proposing that we take a bush taxi. Jean was inscrutable under his new straw hat, a Peul hat which is really very beautiful. However, we arrived in this village of ten huts, with the final discomfort of being without cigarettes. But that resolved the problem of the thing we were there to take care of, to the extent that Mr. Hasseye, as he is known, left in search of one of his friends, a cigarette vendor. Which kept us tied up almost until late afternoon, when Mr. Hasseye came back with the idea of selling us a whole carton of Marlboros. The discussion was extended, in a very pleasant way, until sunset, until we asked if there wasn't a *case de passage*, and Mr. Hasseye took us away from his friend who sells Marlboros. This man is a short Bambara man named Malick, but we are in a Mandinka village. This Mr. Malick lent us a *case de passage* in an isolated hut, and his wife is making us dinner. Sarr Batouly was right to tell us that it was better to stay on the train, because here in the bush you never know what is going to happen. I stop writing because a crowd of savanna dwellers has gathered around me, about ten children and three old people.

17 After a morning fast with Mr. Malick, we continued on the path toward the so-called bus station of Tamba. This, actually, is only a piece of road crowded with ancient modes of transportation, as well as children and young people waiting for lost travelers. Now we're in a Peugeot 404, where it's not uncomfortable with seven, there are even little shades to protect us from the sun, and we're waiting for departure. Jean is somewhat closed up inside himself, the other passengers silent . . . I will always remember the scene from this morning, when Jean resumed his role as leader. In the spasmodic assault of youths and children trying to get hold of us, fighting among themselves, pulling us by the sleeves, I tried to play deaf but I didn't convince them. Jean, instead, raised his hand into the air, right in the middle of the street, making the solemn announcement that if they did not leave us in peace, we would go on foot across the savanna to Dakar. For a second, they were all silent, every one of them in the greatest possible amazement. Then, right away, widespread laughter. The locals split their sides with laughter listening to the bizarre white man who wanted to go on foot across the bush. Luckily that guy with a mature bearing and a white turban came, who kindly suggested to us that it was better if we left by car. Dragged to the car, still however surrounded by an entourage that did not let go of us, it pushed us, it pulled us, it yelled I-don't-know-what to us. Until we were loaded into this Peugeot 404 and immediately they all forgot about us.

18 We cross a zone in the savanna that is full of gigantic termite mounds, two or three meters high, going up into a spire like cathedrals. If they were to be represented in Monet's style, they could be mistaken for cathedrals like the one in Rouen. This ancient automobile seemed to be more satisfactory than some of the others, and its driver immediately seemed to me to be a hero of the savanna. A very handsome man, solidly built, with a blue striped boubou, he had the air of someone who was taking on an enterprise of some weight. A kid drove the car as far as a house with a little store, and the driver came out of there to take his position at the steering wheel, as if a squire had brought him his horse. A ceremony along those lines, maybe the driver had been sleeping. But now I understand his role as an expert in postilion on the frontier, who assumes a certain responsibility on such journeys. Just after fifteen minutes passed, he had to stop to change a flat tire. Then he realized that the spare was fairly flat as well, but a little bit less so, almost passable.

19 Here the land is red again. The road in the bush is larger and the ground packed down hard, almost a real road. All the trees spindly and stunted, not one that stands out from the others. Scattered villages, sometimes with only five or ten grouped huts. Some termite mounds even come to a point, the high point, like a lookout tower on a cliff. Made of gray earth, they spring out of the red earth like fortresses in the desert. Here as well, many tracts of land show traces of a fire, with black earth and singed trees . . . When the crowd in Tamba dragged us by force into the car, there were already other passengers inside, whom I will record here as our travel companions: (1) the Tuareg boy Mohammed El Hez, dressed like a Tuareg who is in keeping with the rules, (2) a plump little Senegalese man who only every so often speaks in French, (3) his so-called big sister, dressed in Western clothing, who travels with a big tin of fresh water, (4) a boy whose head is shaved down to nothing, who was thrown out of France via Bamako, and was going home after two years, without a penny and without papers, with a police record as a delinquent.

20 Many trees in flames along the lane, the ground becomes soot. Perhaps there is spontaneous combustion because of the tremendous heat. Some of these fires are very extensive, shooting out of the screen of trees with high bursts of flames. I wonder if they aren't engulfing villages as well. The scattered villages always have the same types of circular huts made of clay. The only different huts that I have seen are domes of straw, very beautiful and compact, I think it's a Peul style, or maybe I'm imagining it. Many cows in the countryside, beautiful African cows with horns like those in the Maremma, but with full humps at the top of the cervical plexus. Since the Peul are nomadic animal keepers, the most migratory people of Africa, I still have the idea of seeing Peul wandering around with their cows. I'm a little angry with Jean, too, because at Tamba, I would have liked to take the road for the Casamance to travel among the Peul of Fouladou in Guinea Bissau, in search of that nomadic storyteller Diawné Diamanka, to see how he tells stories to his people. Professional curiosity—it would have been educational.

21 The young Tuareg Mohammed El Hez, seated next to the driver, from the time he knew we were Italians has treated us like the closest of friends, because he says that he works a lot with many Italians in Timbuktu. In his wallet he has a bundle of business cards of his clients that he takes by camel into the desert. Among these, many are Italian industrialists whom he calls by first name: Franco, Giuseppe, Aurelio. He's a little perturbed by the fact that we don't have business cards, seeing as we are Italians . . . From time to time, the savanna here is grassland, at times a steppe. Jean, who has seen the Russian steppes, doesn't agree, but it really is a steppe, studded with bare and ghostlike baobab trees, with branches that end in a fist with many fingers, extraordinary trees. Another observation regarding termite mounds, which sometimes reach a height of three and a half meters, a few with central openings that call to mind the cavernous opening of a castle. The sky isn't whitish as usual, but blue, almost turquoise. The desolate savanna—one understands why it's inhabited by evil, starving spirits.

22 After a cluster of huts one of the tires suddenly blew out, but not the one that was a little low, another one in front. Now we're seated on a rock, near a Wolof village; little boys and girls come to examine us with long stares, but without particular reverence. Cevenini and Ridolfi find themselves in places like this on their African journey . . . The village girls have looked at us long enough, they're not interested in us anymore. They go back home, as if they're a little disappointed with the film they've seen. Sitting facing three old men who are chatting beneath a straw canopy roof, looking at one another every so often, that being the polite thing to do, Jean and I cannot say even one word because they speak only Wolof here. Beautiful light of the sunset which announces itself with the first reflections, the shadows that begin to disappear on the ground, while the sky is so huge in these places . . .

23 I would have stayed there forever as well, sitting silently on the rock, dazed, writing. But the blown-out tire required our driver to put the other very deflated tire back on, and he headed toward the regional capital, Kaffrine, in search of help, with the usual good wishes for success: "Inshallah!" Before entering Kaffrine, I notice masses of garbage, which is usually present whenever we get close to a populated center. Its role is different from our garbage dumps. Here, one sees mounds of garbage for half a kilometer, which really are expanses of empty plastic bags no longer containing trash because goats, asses, chickens, dogs and other animals go there in search of food, sweeping clean everything inside the plastic bags. Even the trash is used again: infinite African capacity for makeshift know-how, everything reused in one way or another, from automobile carcasses to domestic trash.

24 Stop at Kaffrine to get the tire repaired, I write sitting on the sidewalk. Mohammed El Hez prays on the rug, the boy thrown out of France tells his story, the small plump one eats a sandwich, his big sister looks for a place to take care of her business, and a little while ago Jean was ticked off at me because I had gone and disturbed him as he drank a Coca-Cola in a very cramped little shop, marvelously overflowing with various items, full of colorful commercial plaques, with a beautiful display of brooms, like in our old pharmacy shops. They told me to go call him, that we were leaving right away, but instead . . .

25 Left Kaffrine about 6:30, with the first shadows. After a little while, another stop in another village because the motor is steaming and there is no water. A matron in a splendid yellow tunic and a matching turban brings us a bucket of water from her hut. We leave again . . . After a few kilometers, stop again, the driver realizes that the radiator is losing water. I witness another miracle of African makeshift know-how. They ask me for a cigarette for the driver, I think he needs to smoke to steady his nerves. Instead, he crumbles it and puts the tobacco into the water tank. With the motion of the water, the tobacco should end up in the hole and block it. In fact, the question of losing water is resolved this way. But right away afterwards, we've got a flat tire. Infinite patience of the driver, true hero of the savanna, he's changing the tire now. Maybe I should insert this trip into the album of textbook cases of African tourism, but someone might believe it's just a novelistic exaggeration.

26 Stopped on the side of a road, heavy darkness, I write by the light of the headlights. Another tire is blown out, after the one we've already changed. Now we're stopped, lacking a second spare. The young Tuareg is muttering: "You can't travel without a supply . . . There are *toubabs* here . . ." El Hez is put out with the driver because there are *toubabs*. He keeps saying that he's making a bad impression on the whites, traveling around without a significant reserve of tires. The driver's calmness in the face of so many nasty complaints, however, impresses me more than the lack of a spare tire . . . Discussions among the passengers in the dark. The small plump one says that he has never had a trip like this. His big sister responds: "We'll be eating at midnight." She has not stopped one second eating and drinking from her vat, that is to say, cooler, the size of a vat. We had to stop in a village to find her some ice, in another to find her some sugar. She gave food and drink to us as well, red currant juice, cookies, fritters . . . The driver tries to flag down passing cars. No one stops. The maternal voice of the big sister enunciates in the dark, a voice that makes calm comments. Now another bush taxi stops, another old Peugeot held together by a miracle. Our driver rushes off in the dark in search of help . . . Discussions on the side of the road, the other driver does not want to lend us his spare tire. They'll send help for us, says the small plump one. A little while ago his big sister asked me where we were going to stay in Dakar. She proposed setting us up at the home of one of her friends. Overbearing kindness, too maternal. Like the time when I had to drink three glasses of sorrel juice because after the second one Jean didn't want anymore. She's named Diop Dabis, she wrote it down for me on a piece of paper, but I'm not sure which is her first name and which is her last name. What should I call her? Madam Diop? Miss Dabis? I'm not unhappy here waiting, as long as Mistress Diop doesn't insist on setting us up in her friend's house.

27 It's the fault of Mistress Diop that we have ended up in this expensive Hôtel Sofitel of Dakar, which, as chance would have it, is a photocopy of the Hôtel de l'Amitié. My pal is gloomy after last night's discussion, the wretched dinner, the tremendously freezing air in the restaurant, where there was a fat and very short businessman accompanied by a very tall black model. There were also two middle-aged European women who ate alone, and three Italian businessmen who were making a big ruckus. When, later, the fat and very short white man was on his way out the door, everyone understood that he was going to go hump the very tall black model. Madness and sadness of the genitals . . . Tonight Jean dreamed that he met a beautiful girl in a soccer stadium, love at first sight, then however he got to know her and said something off, thereby ruining the meeting, with great disappointment: "That girl represents all the fantasizing I have done on the documentary about the Bamako-Dakar train, which then turned out poorly . . ." Last evening at dinner we almost quarreled, because I was finding him to be too disappointed and he was ruining my contentment at just wandering around haphazardly. There outside, this city of Dakar looks like Milan, with its penthouses with hanging gardens and antennae, while when we arrived at the outskirts, it looked like Naples to me. From my window, the view of apartment blocks and balconies and palm trees could be Palermo. Gray-blue sky.

28 I have just telephoned Sarr Batouly to get back the pullover and other things that Jean had forgotten on the train. Point number one: I understand that Sarr is her last name, Batouly is her first name. Point number two: she proposes bringing us Jean's things this evening, but she will have to take a taxi because she lives out of the way. "We can't come to your house?" Impossible, she says, because you simply cannot get there, even by taxi, if you don't know the places. Given that she's being inconvenienced to come here from so far away, I suggest we have dinner together. She says: "Can I bring a girlfriend?" So, this evening dinner with Batouly and her pal. Jean is afraid that we will find ourselves in the situation of the very short white man from last night, the one who was going to hump the very tall model. This particular take on things puts me in ill humor. His lack of desire at the idea of meeting with these young black women. To resolve the situation, I propose that he stay at the Sofitel and I go to dinner with the two of them. Among other things, we're in this situation because of him, he's the one who forgot his pullover on the train.

29 Four o'clock by the side of the pool at this horrendous Hôtel Sofitel. Pool with that dark blue from publicity photos, big exotic straw canopies. The white women expose breasts to the sun, the black attendants bring drinks to the small tables. We talk about Jean's documentary, now contrived to be in keeping with Thomas Harlan's notions. I recommend a documentary on Boubacar, with filming on the high plain to show his art as a walker, but also on what goes on as a tourist guide (this trade is an almost mythological one for the youths we have met, and it is their way of integrating themselves into the territory, instead of fleeing to the city and going out of their minds.) Then I suggest putting Boubacar on the Bamako-Dakar train, having him tell stories about the Dogon kids who flee to the city, and at the same time, filming the savanna. From there, on the train, you would meet: whom? The well-known German director Thomas Harlan, with his itinerant company of actors, who stop to perform Shakespeare's *Tempest* . . . Utmost relaxation by tourists in lounge chairs, sunset is coming. Two American ladies here on the side, chirping away, with that tone of being-satisfied-with-everything that is peculiar to Americans: admirable and nice blue-haired ladies. We rethink our trip, which has brought us here instead of to the Casamance, and no one knows why.

SEVENTH NOTEBOOK

1 Dakar. This morning, trip around the Place de l'Indépendence, saw the French colonial houses, and in front of us
the island de N'gor, where we will soon go. Yesterday evening
with Batouly and her friend Bindou, dinner at Fouquets.
Batouly showed up with what seemed to be an irritated expression and without Jean's pullover. Ate couscous with fish. I cannot describe the iciness. But on the train we were such good
friends! Sure, but none of us was in our own territory there, here
it all changes. The only moment when she spoke willingly was
when she talked about her marriage, venting about her husband
who used to beat her. Then she angrily said to me: "I am jealous,
I am!" But I don't know why she said it, we're not at all involved
in any kind of romantic thing. To top it all off, a combo of
African musicians showed up at the place, and they came and
went through the room with utmost calm, leaving a few behind
to keep playing the same Brazilian songs. One was supposed to
dance—myself, certainly not, but Jean was obliged in that he
knew how to salsa dance.

2 On the Avenue Georges Pompidou, assaults by vendors
galloping along after us, aside from those who are station-
ary on the two sidewalks. Now a blind man on the ground fills the
crowded street with his piercing cries at the top of his lungs, he
speaks of Allah and no one pays any attention to him. In the

Café de Paris, the French owner wearing a red turban is doing her receipts, we're the only ones in the place. The blind man seated on the sidewalk is no longer wailing, he has started to sing. Here, the trade of the blind is always that of the singer. We have seen a great many of them, including the blind boy at Tamba, dressed in white, with a sack slung over his shoulders, a voice like a flute . . . Observations about when eyes meet on the street: here I do not see spying glances like in England, nor of sizing things up as in Italy, but often it is as if one is coming over to shake your hand, then at the last second veers off. In a European city, many walk without looking at anyone, but these people have the look of serious, busy professionals . . . Another blind singer passes by with his hand on the shoulder of a little boy, and he sings a very sad lamentation, while the little boy sticks his fingers up his nose. In the heavy traffic the cars move at a crawl, amidst the colors, the dust, the crowd, the merchandise on the sidewalks, the vendors of everything imaginable. The whites who pass all have a stiff way of walking and wandering eyes, while the locals proceed with quick bursts of sideways glances. After an hour, the wailing blind man has not been given one donation, he screams in the name of Allah and no one pays any attention to him.

3 By the side of the Sofitel pool, I witness a quarrel between the black attendants. The infuriated supervisor speaks in French to a subordinate, who answers him in Wolof. Speaking in Wolof, the others try to help ease the altercation, but the supervisor is still ranting in French to the one who has infuriated him. ("Do what I say, period!") In his rage, he uses French as the official language of authority. The others, who are speaking Wolof, turn everything into a joke, they cannot remain serious. This is how we use languages: some are used to take on the tone of authority, others to abolish the arrogance of serious, weighty words . . . Today Jean went to the island of Gorée, the point from which the shiploads of slaves departed, and where there is now a museum about the slaves. When I went with him, all those who were crowded together for boarding were enthusiastically chatting, no one showed any sign of being in a hurry, the whole crowd prattled on with great enjoyment. The pleasure of talking on and on is evident here, but as I understand it, the ultimate pleasure is in chatting away in Wolof, sprinkled with French words, so as to lose the woodenness of the official language and bring liveliness to the way of speaking. On the landing pier, there was a group of Americans as well, and they were the only ones who were quiet while waiting for the ferry. The one that stood out among them was the elderly leader, dressed in hunting clothes, a broad-brimmed leather hat, a necklace of panther teeth, he lacked only a big-game hunting rifle—he too was coming to see the slave museum.

4 This morning I called Batouly; friendly again, she invited us to dinner at her house. I don't know why she was so morose at Fouquets, perhaps because our worries were hanging over everything there, Jean looking for cultural explanations, myself with my head somewhere else. Maybe she couldn't figure it out: what types are we? There's a lot to learn here . . .

5 About noon we take a walk toward the port. On the Boulevard de la Libération, the market with stalls of every imaginable thing, cloth, sandals, meat grinders, milk in cartons, lightbulbs, razor blades, stacks of all different kinds of canned food, big baskets with cassette tapes of music. Then immediately after this market, which one is hardly able to pass through, between the female vendors seated on the ground, the idle old people shuffling their slippered feet, the ladies who stand there assessing their purchases, the workers leaning against the wall who are smoking, right after this, two boys approach me. One wants to sell me a bracelet, the other I don't know what. I press onward, but the one with the bracelet stays right behind me, puts a hand on my shoulder to stop me. I see the other who is blocking my left side, but I don't pay any attention to him. However, in the meantime, the one in back of me is squeezing my shoulder until it hurts, so hard that I let out a howl to free myself from his grip. Immediately after the hysterical yell, the two boys run off like hares. An old taxi driver with a gray beard tells me to check to see if I still have everything, and I see the pouch with the money and papers is open. The one on the side had pulled open the zipper and was in the process of robbing me, while the other was distracting me with the painful gripping of my shoulder.

6 At dinner, Batouly said that Dakar is full of *voyous*, hoodlums, we must be careful! She took us under her protection as far as the train, we must listen to her. At any rate, after the assault on the Boulevard de la Libération, the old taxi driver had advised me to walk on the other sidewalk where some workers were loading a pile of dusty and smelly trash onto a truck, yawning and calmly talking in the cloud of dust. Nearby on the sidewalk, a woman was selling oranges, sitting on the ground and surrounded by the same cloud of dust; others spread out on the pavement slept peacefully as I traveled along that toxic sidewalk. But we, who put a great deal of importance on distinguishing between humanity and garbage, should stop, enchanted by this indolence, by this lazy tendency of neatly isolating inner man from the garbage of the world. I make note, as well, that from the moment of the assault, for me the inner was clearly the money in my money-pouch, and the outer all the rest that I can and cannot buy with this money. For my assailants, instead, like maenads emerging from the clouds of trash, it's a question of abolishing the separation between the inner and the outer which is what lets stand our privacy as civilized people. However, I played my part quite well, and with one hysterical yell, I did not allow them to clean me out.

7 More or less in a daze after the evening of partying with Batouly, her friend Bindou, and the third friend, Coumba, who cannot resist the demon of dancing for even one evening. I need to stay in seclusion after these exhausting nighttime get-togethers in the bar Dakar, modeled in the Parisian style, with a Rastafarian reggae singer, with the Senegalese DJ who talks like

Sartre and gives publicity plugs, with the drunk who always wants to hook up with our group, without mentioning the too-warm welcome at Fouquets by that famous, elastic-bodied singer, mustache like a conquistador, smooth voice, who dedicates all the Brazilian songs to us. In these encounters, I feel like I've tumbled back into my student years. Jean makes anthropological comments. Batouly grumbles angrily about Dakar, and yesterday evening, as she danced for a moment I saw her body in broken-up pieces, as if she had many pieces that would not hold together. One piece even slipped into the doorway, then once in the spectral entryway, it didn't know which way to go anymore.

8 Ordinary encounters near the Place de l'Indépendence: (1) some guy who insisted on selling me a pair of sunglasses, never mind that I was wearing one, something that did not concern him one bit; (2) the boy who wanted to sell me an American newspaper from last week, already read and, just for good measure, muddy; (3) the one who wanted to give me a *grigri*, but for a payment, saying that it is a magical amulet made by his sorcerer grandfather, and then he put it on my shoulder with the warning that I shouldn't be afraid of it, otherwise something bad would happen; (4) the little boy who offered me a cassette of the most famous Senegalese singer, but when I explained to him that I wasn't interested, he burst out laughing as if I had told an improbable cock-and-bull story: "That's not true, you're just kidding!" (5) the youth who said that he had just come back from Milan and found it unbelievably hilarious as soon as he learned that I'm Italian, and then low-fives to say that we're friends and we should go together to Cape Skiring next week. Then he suddenly went off, saying: "I'll call you!" But where?

9 Batouly's house is located in a maze of narrow unnamed streets, in the Sicap quarter, beyond the Medina, inaccessible without a guide. Courtyard life there is very intense and goes on until after midnight, with the coming and going of neighbors and other people you don't know. One face after another pops in, says hello and disappears, like in a piazza. Which is why it's difficult to tell who's in the family and who's not. I'll reconstruct what I understand about the Sarr household and those who live around the courtyard: (1) Batouly, the only one in the family who has work; (2) her two children, had with the husband who beat her, from whom she is separated; (3) her sister, Hélène, younger, doing nothing because she can't find work; (4) a third sister, Marie, who wasn't there, but normally lives there, out of work; (5) the mother whom I only caught a glimpse of because she was always slipping away; (6) Coumba, who lives in the same courtyard, immediately very friendly, thin and very lively, she too out of work and she too with (7) two children from a preceding husband; and, in addition, (8) the tall and very black man, a Diola from the Casamance, a traveling salesman, for whom Coumba prepares meals in the evening like a wife, then he goes to sleep in the same courtyard, while Coumba goes out dancing at night; (9) Batouly's Rastafarian brother, a singer who lived in Paris where he has a thriving reggae Wolof group, permanently dulled by marijuana, and with a permanently frozen smile, now come back to Dakar for a month to make a video, together with (10) his wife, a small Parisian, who criticizes everything in the Sarr home and always goes around with a bottle of sterilized water, absolute groupie of her singer husband. When I ask her what kind of work she does, she replies with self-importance: "I'm in perfume."

10 Everything's going well, I'm liking everything, but I need to be by myself in seclusion to think and to write. For that reason, we're going to the island of N'gor . . . In the Sofitel lobby everything moves in accordance with strict maps, as if each person has a particular route to the reception desk, to the bar, to the elevators. There is no space here for the rambling idleness one sees on the street. The white man wants to travel in a straight line, and usually keeps in control of the situation with ninety-degree surveillance glances. But in this traffic, regulated by a rigorous system of signs ("Reception," "Cashier," "Information,"

"Restaurant," "Pool"), whites show a remarkable stiffness when they move straight ahead and a lack of composure when they turn. The rambling Africans I see on the street are never flustered, and they have the gift of the sideways glance in instantaneous little bursts, with a flexible turn of the neck. It is precisely because whites always have the problem of keeping control of situations that the Africans' loose rambling is impossible for them, and in situations that are scarcely controllable, they adopt the stopgap measure of keeping *themselves* rigidly under control. For whites here, it's a question of walking on the stilts of their egos right in the middle of the black multitude, which does not have that problem and which sniffs out the whites' teetering equilibrium, ready to make good use of it to extract a few pennies from them.

11 In the lobby of the Sofitel, the only thing that attracts me is a life-size, indigenous wooden sculpture in front of the terrace door. Beautiful sculpture that comes from the Casamance, I think, and represents the white man as explorer, outfitted with an explorer's hat, hunting rifle, shorts of the tourist on vacation. It's a figure that captures the comic essence of the white man. Because whites always have an air about them saying: "Everything's under control, I'm calm, you see?" They say it with glances, with clothing, with cars, with the shorts worn on vacation, with all the signs of fashion, or else with the hunting rifle. But the anxiety of keeping situations under control makes almost all of them comical or flustered, always worried about a map, a legal code, a future project, about the nostalgia for a past, never here in the vague present of any old moment. Maybe it is their nature, like that of birds, some more agitated than others, some lighter, some heavier, but each obligated to take those flights as if they were following their illusions.

12 Arrived on the island of N'gor. Not very fascinating island of lavic rock, in seclusion in the pension, Chez Carla, an Italian lady married to a Senegalese. We did not see much of

Dakar, it's a big city . . . Coming here, the taxi driver drove slowly along the coastal road, then he had to make the trip all the way back and recross half the city because Jean had forgotten his Peul hat at the hotel, but didn't want to have to pay more than the agreed-upon price. To top it off, on the Avenue Roumé, a car came up behind us, crushing a fender and scurrying away as if nothing had happened. The taxi driver got out to study the crushed fender, he stayed there for a little while in the middle of traffic, then he got back into the car without even a single complaint. He is one of the most serenely resigned men I have seen in recent years. In contrast, as soon as we got out of the taxi, a group of kids assailed us so they could take us to a boat, these people not the least bit resigned to our refusals. They were led by a more adult-looking type with a baseball cap, who pulled me by the sleeve, and I said to him: "Leave me the hell alone!" At which he became offended and protested my indelicate expression. I tried to be resigned myself, apologizing a lot, but he would not accept my excuses. Right away, he seized upon my expression of resignation and immediately exploited it by pulling me again by the sleeve with the intention of taking us to a boat that was exorbitantly priced. I weakly protested but he said: "No, no, it's not expensive!" still pulling me by the sleeve in the middle of that cortège of ragtag little kids. In the meantime, we had arrived at the beach and here we found Signora Carla (the proprietor of our little pension, short, plump, dressed without fuss, with the brisk, businesslike manner of Milan), who with four yells put the pack of kids to flight. But she made the one with the baseball cap load cartons of mineral water, produce, poultry, fish, various kinds of boxes onto the boat, then she chased him away with a brusque gesture, and he obeyed her as if he were a schoolboy. During the brief crossing of the inlet, this energetic Signora Carla told us practically her whole life's story, the different restaurants she has had, her specialities in Italian home cooking, she even talked about the climate and fishing and her customers, and about the fact that she has had malaria four times but she has never taken to bed to recuperate, not even one day.

13 From here one can see Dakar's coastal road. Now the Sum Makara pirogue comes back to shore, with three tourists and three of those kids who pounced on us yesterday. In the middle of the inlet, a yacht is pitched, where they say there's a moored German musician. Offshore the big waves attract surfers. In this place, the room is very humid, the water too cold . . . I haven't made note of the best moments in the Sarr house, when the women talked among themselves, seated on the ground, happy, very happy, with alternating voices as if they were singing: soprano voice of that neighbor from Gabon, mezzo-soprano Coumba who told that story in Wolof, miming it, and I thought it was a funny story but instead it was about a funeral. Afterwards, Batouly showed us photographs, a sign of being accepted into the family—but I remember most of all the few torn and creased photos of her father, leading figure in the Senegalese Communist party, who lived in Prague and Paris, displayed like the remnants of the family's treasure. At home she changes completely, because she is a little bit the head of the family, everything is under her wings, the adult sister with a job. The courtyard is her territory, but outside that territory, Dakar, for her, is hell. So when she thinks about it, she becomes a snared beast, and she grumbles irascibly, and goes to pieces. In the face of cases like this, the European tourist is at a loss, as if in a state of siege behind his protective glass.

14 Bewildering night from the cold and humidity on the island of N'gor. This morning, on a walk on fly-infested paths, among horrid little houses abandoned and overgrown by weeds, this slender boy who called himself Zorro approached me ("My name is Zorro like in the movies"). He introduced himself as the head of the guides for visits to the island (altogether, there are three little streets), and he says that he intends to take me to see Georges Pompidou's villa (it doesn't exist), but he doesn't want money because friendship is more valuable than money. ("Money gets eaten up, relationships endure.") He adds that he is also a poet and has published books of poetry (same things recited to Jean), and he immediately started to recite one of them (the same one recited to Jean), which consisted of a long prosopopoeia of welcome to the island, full of laudatory adjectives ("Honorable are you who come, I respect you because you are dignified . . .") as well as solemn wishes for my happiness during my stay ("May your eyes sparkle with joy . . ."). Then when I accelerated, he followed along in a run, suggesting that I was a very nice type of person, he could see it right away, and not like my buddy (he said Jean was cheap), therefore, he intended to show me the villa of a French singer named Françoise Gall (on whose various marriages he expounded), until, collaring me again near Chez Carla, he suggested that if I didn't want to give him any money, I should give him at least a pair of pants or a tee shirt as payment for the visit to the island.

15 On this suffocatingly hot day, with the harmattan blowing from land, I took up the story of Cevenini and Ridolfi again. Wrote until noon . . . Afternoon. For the series of textbook cases of African tourism, a picture of the situation from this area will fit very nicely. The tourist, red as a lobster from the African sun, goes to see the slave museum on the island of Gorée; he's even happy, of course, that the slave trade doesn't exist anymore, but then going out he meets one like Zorro who stuns him with his steady prattle that will go on until he pulls out some change from his pocket for him, while here on the beach the whites buy blacks, and you see the cripple with the black child, the ancient European with the African youth, all types of promiscuity readily offered for a fee. Nothing escapes the human-flesh traffic between white and blacks, but I am running short of moral judgments.

16 Whitish sky near the earth, gray-blue up high. Tomorrow we're going to St. Louis. We'll wait on the seashore until the tide is high enough for the boat to leave. A cormorant in front of us on the rocks looks about, not a single tourist wandering around. Batouly calls because she wants us to see one another right away. When we announced our departure to her, she was even jealous, asked if we were here with women, stuff of wives or girlfriends on tenterhooks . . . Jean's wandering around thinking about a plan for his documentary. I'm writing long-hand, because I wanted to start writing again by hand, and the travel journal is good for that. I would like to write a eulogy for writing by hand, even if it's just to say that the tide is slowing entering into the small cove of volcanic rock, and the sun is encircled by whitish cirrus clouds and that everything around it is opaque. Even just to pass time, without being in a hurry, letting time grow intertwined with sentences that come a few at a time, while the boy sweeps the patio and I look at the immobility of the cormorants.

17 Morning, 9:30. Dakar bus station, in search of a bus to St. Louis. On arrival, they all swarmed us as usual, pulling us in different directions, until a stronger little group prevailed and took possession of us. I left it to my leader Jean, who dealt with it beautifully. In fact, they immediately loaded us, like two beasts being transported I don't know where, onto this wreck of a bus, nearly empty, which will leave who knows when. Then, right off, the ticket seller sells us tickets, we are prisoners and cannot change buses. This one, however, has special decorations, I see, with many photos of important religious figures and politicians above the driver's seat, like a display of protective saints above a little altar. The nearby horizon line is an expanse of other buses, more or less falling apart like ours, and the ground is a vast clay deposit where everything is mixed in with mud, which today is wet, pieces of paper, plastic bottles, a broken sandal, little piles of yellow stuff, charred remnants, fragments of polystyrene . . .

18 Ten o'clock. They are starting to set up their merchandise in the line of booths in front of us. Some of the vendors are talking calmly under the shade of their big umbrellas, others sleep, others smoke, seated in front of a little shed with a caved-in roof. It is only we who were victims of the morning's workday frenzy that broke out among the ones who dragged us here, then immediately disappeared, leaving us alone on this bus. Jean maintains that they even made us pay more than the others, a tax for *toubabs,* that is to say, for white *pingoni,* as he says. But now we have paid, we can't turn back, and this bus will leave only when it's full of people. For now, it's only us and two other silent ones. On the door of the little shed facing us, a sign says ICI COIFFEUR, but there's nothing behind the door, the little hut ends there.

19 A very black gentleman arrives, pulling a goat behind him, attached by a cord on its leg, so that it must hop around on three hooves, it falls and rises from the mud, while the owner discusses how it will be loaded onto the roof of the bus. Jean gets off and on, bringing me news about the most recent theories: when will the bus be filled? at what time will we leave? I am elaborating on a new subject for his documentary. I'm thinking about a documentary on a bus like this one, which will leave no one knows when, about two *toubabs* waiting in the Dakar bus station. I don't tell him about it, but I make notes for his future cinematographic undertaking, which will be a sure success.

20 Eleven-thirty. Only three other passengers have arrived. Outside the bus, there's a banana vendor who's shouting, one man who convinced Jean to give him 500 CFA for no reason at all, and another who's wandering around with a display of photos of singers, actors, political figures, religious leaders, attached to a portable signboard. Behind me, a transistor turned all the way up talking about the latest African rap production. Interview with a new African rap group. The head of the group: "Yes, for us life is all an apprenticeship..." He says that his group is inspired by another group, that is by another group leader, and this other leader of the other group is named Daraji, if my ears are working well: "New reality ... the philosophy of Harun al Daraji...plural music..." Now the head of the group introduces the latest cassette produced by his rap group, declaring that it is specially dedicated to the Senegalese public. I ask myself to whom else it could have possibly been dedicated. But he explains the subtle question: "It is necessary to say clearly that making music and making sense are two different things. Our music should not interest just young people. There is a linguistic base, it's necessary that people know it . . ." The others in the group spoke like professors as well. Their music is a little rancid, I'm saying this respectfully. But everything's moving along in this big Dakar bus station, racket and calm confusion, nonsense and marvels for a tourist who's in no hurry to leave. Four other passengers arrive.

21 Twelve-thirty. The bus is still very empty. In the meantime, I make note that the stalls in front of us have not yet had a single customer. On display there are oil lamps, plastic aprons, little African necklaces, rubber slippers, Adidas shoes, colorful polystyrene basins, coffee grinders, brooms made of sorghum, leaflets from the Koran, wrenches, baby clothes, together with boxes of coffee and tomatoes. There's everything there, the world's great variety, including the vendors who sleep stretched out on their merchandise. They really know how to sleep here. This is something to desire, forget about conquest of the planet.

22 One-thirty. Someone says that maybe we will have to wait until five. "It depends on the customers . . ." Discussions among the passengers who are waiting. For a half hour now, the radio has been airing an interview of a very old man with an angry voice, an incensed religious leader. I do not understand if he is for or against the Muslim practice of having many wives, because he says that he has only one, he praises their life together, he declares that he has never been with another woman, but he says it with so much anger as if he's unhappy about it. A line of vendors who come up onto the bus offering everything, one is selling razor blades, one sells pepper and other spices, one brushes and brooms. Now the radio is airing an interview with another important figure armed with pedagogy, nasal voice and certainty in his breast: "Everything that I am saying is one hundred percent authenticated, so it is necessary to listen to me as an authenticated man . . ." (word for word). Then I am distracted because someone enters who wants to sell me a pennant of the soccer team Inter, or else photos of the players on Inter, whatever you want . . .

23 Two-thirty. The bus is filling up. Odor of urine from the window, at times the odor of fish. Jean declares that this wait is hallucinatory, but he does not know about the documentary I'm writing for him. A woman of true Wolof beauty has sat down in front of us, who looks like the famous queen Taitù, with extraordinary elegant clothing with purple stripes, turban of the same material, two ritualistic scars between temples and eyebrows, hair in dreadlocks tightly clinging to her head, brown skin that makes a beautiful contrast with the white bra and the fine white underpants visible through the side opening of her dress. Outside the bus, there is a sea of heads, a hodgepodge of humanity, through which two men are carrying an iron bed, holding it up high, but they're blocked. This Queen Taitù is a magnificent actress, and it would be necessary to make friends with her, because if we could have her in our documentary, we would be lucky. But she is very proud, you see that she feels like a queen, she keeps her distance from everyone. The other side of it is that she is also an irresistible Circe and she wants to assert her charm. Earlier, with smiles and flirting, she negotiated the ticket price with the ticket seller who looks like a Chicago bookmaker, but in the end she wound up paying as much as the others.

24 Three-thirty. The harmattan blows, it's necessary to close the windows. I make note that the gentleman with the goat has succeeded in loading it on top of another bus, where the goat, all wrapped up in a fishing net, is using its horns to try to extricate itself, but it's also tied and looks like a strange sea animal. Now we are tuned into Radio Senegal, news from all around: at the bus station in St. Louis, a Malian stabbed a Senegalese man,

the mob lynched him . . . A gentleman in a gray boubou got off
a little bit ago with a cardboard box, and now we find out that inside the box there are two chickens which have an unadulterated
African accent: "Ko-ko-kò . . ." It's very hot, and hotter still as
the bus fills up. Still six empty seats, but they will have to fill even
the folding seats in the middle aisle, my neighbor dressed in
Western clothes informs me.

25 The folding seats filled, we are trapped and unable to move
from our seats. Queen Taitù, however, continues with her
seductive witticisms and tittering, discussing the price of a
household broom that a vendor is showing her, after having
passed through the bodies in the middle folding chairs. In the
end, she buys the broom . . . Four-thirty. Now it should be time
to leave, but we find out that they have to load certain drainpipes
onto the bus's roof, pipes that have been lying on the ground
since our arrival. Jean says that he does not understand why they
didn't load them sooner, and I agree with him. It's hard to
understand as well why, instead of loading them, they stand
around discussing it, tranquilly lighting cigarettes, and turn
around to chat with people who pass by, and the most brawny one
of the bunch assigned to do the lifting has now gone to pee,
squatting down on the ground near the corner of our bus.

26 Finally the bus is moving through the throng of vendors
who are knocking on the windows. However, it is blocked
by the customers who are running en masse toward the stalls,
right at this moment, after six hours of total absence. The driver,
a little old man in a red *cecìa,* indifferent to the crowd, doesn't
even honk the horn. He has to get gas at the bus station exit, another
stop. Behind us, a view of buses as far as the eye can see, the un-
limitedness of the world, where certainly God is in every unique
and imperfect thing, as one of my characters, sister Tran, said.

27 The sky is wrapped up in reddish veils, the harmattan is
blowing hard, after Rufisque we go against the wind. A

police roadblock along the way, bus stopped, vendors who jump up to the windows trying to sell us fruits and vegetables. A half hour later, 5:30, stopped again, this time for prayers. Many get off the bus and kneel on rugs with their heads on the ground. My pal gets off to anxiously smoke, cursing their praying and even Allah, then apologizes, explaining that we have spent one entire day to go thirty kilometers. I tell him he's right, but it's a little false, I'm lying a bit. I still don't want to talk to him about the documentary I'm in the process of writing for him. During the prayers, Queen Taitù goes around a corner to take care of her business, then she comes back adjusting her underwear in plain view of four delighted men who, from the start of the trip, have been appreciating and courting her from their fixed positions.

28 Seven o'clock, stopped in Louga. The usual blind man comes up to sing, but this one isn't blind at all, only blind in one eye; to make up for it, he has a paralyzed hand that looks like a baobab branch. Jean, who's gotten off, finds himself surrounded by small children who insistently ask to drink some of his Coca-Cola. They unload the famous drainpipes and throw down the baggage of the travelers who are getting off in Louga. They mistakenly throw down our backpacks as well, but before giving them back to us the supervisor wants to see the tickets. And here I discover that the Chicago bookmaker gave me just one ticket, making me pay for two, I hadn't realized it. Luckily the superintendent isn't a stickler for fiscal regularity and he gives me his blessing.

29 Eight o'clock. In the shadows of the bus in front of me, Queen Taitù continues to hold court, directing chit-chat and giggles to the men around her, one in particular at her shoulder, a skinny and suspicious-looking guy in the folding chair next to her, who, for an hour, does not hesitate to rub himself against her and eagerly touch her thigh, while tossing off joking words. This is an unforgettable spectacle, because the carnal voracity of the sleazy fellow is treated by the queen as a simple excess of hilarity. It's true that she sometimes puts his hand back in its place, but without discomposure, without even looking at the groping movements that reach her in the dark. She must also entertain three males in the next row who are paying court. She is a Circe who holds everyone under her spell, therefore she cannot be distracted and lose control of the situation. A little while ago, the queen asked me for my fountain pen, putting an arm behind, a fleshy and commanding arm, but without turning around, as if I were a page in her retinue. Then she had the light inside the bus turned on, and she wrote down her address and telephone number for her various admirers.

30 Nine o'clock. Jean has found something to talk about with a girl who got on at Louga. Queen Taitù gets off at night at a group of huts, taking along the broom she bought and various other packages. Who knows where she lives? Who knows whether her husband gave her the luxurious arm bracelet with embedded stones? We did not get to know her and we have lost her for our documentary, I'm very, very sorry. I have nothing more to write for today.

EIGHTH NOTEBOOK

1 Hôtel Résidence, St. Louis. Good sleep, despite the noise and the perpetual muezzin who was singing. Colonial hotel that feels like a ship inside. As in all colonial situations, one lives in a ghetto of whites. I miss the bus from yesterday, but the idea is proceeding about the documentary on a bus that never leaves the Dakar bus station, with two Europeans who little by little calm down and are never in a hurry again for the rest of their lives . . . St. Louis reminds me of New Orleans, in the style of the streets, shape of the houses, colors. I again find a piece of architecture that I have seen only in New Orleans, the Creole balconies of the French Quarter . . . A long strip of land in the middle of the Senegal River; the bridge that connects it to the interior is made of iron, from the turn of the century, with four arches. We walk aimlessly along the shore as far as the ocean, led by a guy met on the street named Babà, I don't know if that's the first or last name, and he offers himself as a tour guide to accompany us to Mauritania. I do know that the spell of travel is becoming even weaker, but I don't even want to know why we have come here.

2 Morning, Sunday. We walk along the Rue Ibrahim Sarr, completely empty except for us and two women on the step of a house. Beautiful silent streets, with two-story houses, flat roofs, pale colors on the facades, an air of colonial relaxation. Cross-streets full of artisan boutiques: Coiffeur, Couturier,

Plumber, Cobbler. I would like to inspect them one by one, but Jean wants to visit the cinematographic center created by a Jesuit with a passion for film (Daniel Blottier), near the hospital. As soon as we set foot in the atrium, a man invites us to enter the room where there's a lecture; we follow him without knowing what it's about. A young woman dressed in Western clothing talks to an assembly of women in colorful skirt-cloths and tunics, stating the arguments in French, then elaborating on them in Wolof. In French she is extremely serious, with professorial language, but when she speaks in Wolof, she laughs easily and makes her listeners laugh. She talks about the situation of women, about their education and their relationships with husbands. "We want respect and tranquillity . . ." The listeners laugh, nodding their heads to say she's right, one of them looks at us to try to figure out who we are. It's a kind of assembly against domineering African husbands.

3 After the gathering of women, I think of Batouly's story about the house where she stayed in Bamako: there was a man with four wives, each with her turn of conjugal rights, but each one had a lover she tranquilly visited in her free time. This is what Batouly said, who abhors Muslim polygamy, as do many women. But she didn't seem to me equally condemning of the opposite tendency, the voluptuous intrigues with different men, bawdy courtships and immediately lots of sex, collective seductions, sexual bantering without restraint, promiscuous entanglements, enraged female jealousies, male thwacks, voluntary separations. It's necessary to say as well that Cevenini and Ridolfi are often bewildered by African loves.

4 Obsessed by St. Louis, I proposed to Jean forgetting about all the other ideas and making a documentary on the streets of St. Louis. While we were walking on the Rue de France, on two little side streets there were chairs set up, with people sitting in them who were amiably talking in the middle of the street, in a big display of silk and colorful clothing. One

must have been a baptism, the other a wedding. It was the most elaborate exhibition of festive clothing that I had seen on this trip, but the colors of the material would perhaps have been excessive, were it not for the bearing of effortless self-possession I admire so much. Farther ahead, going down the Rue Ababacar, a woman who was picking lice off her son on the step of a house, goats who were eating banana peels, a woman who was cooking fish over coals on the street, a man who was grazing his herd of sheep in a little alleyway, a coal seller who was shoveling wearing an antismog mask . . . Then the line of trees on either side of the Avenue Mermoz, the French consulate, the goats foraging through trash, the shade of the great acacia trees, tamarisks, eucalyptus bushes. Heading toward the sea, small, barely sketched-out houses in pastel colors, old French houses wrapped in bougainvillea, the firefighters' barracks, the silence of empty lanes and the harmattan. On the island's bridge, the wind shook the palm trees behind us with this sound: "Shooh-it, shooh-it." Nearby, the courtyard of an abandoned French house was a mysterious place. A man alone on a bench looked at the sea. Until a sports utility vehicle of Americans came roaring in, and the American woman, without getting out, filmed everything.

5   Some more notes about Sunday's walk. In front of the island's tip, pirogues with veils, herons in the distance, to the right a swath of palm trees sticking up which perhaps is the Mauritanian border. The enormously large mouth of the Senegal River, with the Langue de Barbarie peninsula, the Barbary Coast, on one side. What names from novels! Going back a radio could be heard that aired political announcements, there were clothes hung out in the lanes, a huge billy goat tied up. Then a soccer field without grass, but with the regulation lines marked on asphalt, so empty and silent that we were spellbound looking at it. Afterwards, stop in the postcard seller's shop, a young man with an accountant's gestures, with fussy precision toward the customer, seated behind a very well ordered table, beneath a sign that said NO SMOKING PLEASE, then farther

above the portrait of the president of Senegal. His shop was very orderly as well, everything painted an emerald color, with two pay-phone booths, the door with screened windows made of colorful raffia fronds, and three chairs the same emerald color as the walls, a very beautiful den to film. And again on the Rue Ababacar, an emporium from another time, with old wooden shutters on the windows, plaques with various commercial trademarks, overlapped by the poster LACOSTE ET CIE, on a street of two-story colonial houses, pastel-colored walls, no one out and about at that hour of the day, not even one car driving around, like a Sunday miracle. Back in the hotel, Jean started watching the soccer match on television, without even listening to my proposals for a documentary on the streets of St. Louis.

6 The adventures of Cevenini and Ridolfi proceed, I started writing about them again this morning . . . Call to Batouly, who has a troubled voice. Her teeth are bothering her, one dentist wants to pull out five of them, and she asks: when are we coming back? She would have come to St. Louis with us, she says, if only we had asked her to. I see her again in detached pieces that will not stay together, one goes here, one goes there. I even dreamed about it. I don't understand what it means when someone in Dakar says, "I am nostalgic for you." It is not a sentimental appeal, our own romanticism doesn't enter into it, genitals either. However, I cannot manage to translate the rest of it, which is perhaps an appeal for help. Because we are "family," as she says? But the dazed tourist is without family, he too is made of detached pieces, one going here, one going there. At a certain point it could be that he will no longer be able to see his shadow that is walking beside him.

7 In this hotel there are many attendants with such small tasks that I don't understand what they're doing here. For example, the guy in braided uniform whom I find in front of my room every day, I have the impression that his only task is to dust the railing, because I see him making only this motion. Another with the same uniform sweeps only the landing, but for hours, slowly. The woman who looks after the restaurant at breakfast time disappears after nine. There's a different face at the reception desk every hour. The restaurant waiters, costumed like skirmishers in the colonial army, appear only at peak times. They wear pants with large puffs, while the French owner is dressed as if he's going to play polo or cricket, and the black doorman has a uniform like an American police officer. There's a general atmosphere of masquerade, and it seems that everyone comes to put in a small appearance, with a rapid turnover, then he runs to hide. But yesterday evening an event brought out all the personnel, because a huge mouse emerged in the dining room, he had escaped into the bar, then he had hidden I don't know where. So for the first time I verified the existence of two elegant bartenders in traditional outfits, who gave off desperate shouts standing on the bar. Then I saw that our smiling, tubby waiter exists during the day as well, because he came running in with a broom. The one who dusts the railing showed up as well, with a drowsy expression. The morning person on the reception desk arrived carrying a cat, which, however, wanted nothing to do with it, and scatted. And many others emerged from their lairs or hiding places, where perhaps they were sleeping, waiting for their turn to perform. So many people that it seemed like a party, chatting about the mouse, laughing and dispersing, satisfied because of the exceptional event.

8   Vendors selling knickknacks are stationed in front of the hotel, but without the massive assaults that daze, because each has his assigned section of sidewalk. The hangers-on at the reception desk, on the other hand, have their own traffic to maintain, and they willingly chase away their outside rivals, then suggest to the customers where they must buy things, how to rent a car, how to go on a trip, always telephoning a friend. In the end, the approaches by the knickknack vendors just outside the hotel's door are regulated by a very tall doorman, with a huge stomach, dressed like an American policeman from his boots to

his Ray-Ban sunglasses. This one, yesterday, leaning toward me, whispering, asked me for 500 CFA. I asked: "Why?" He, voice lowered, shady-looking: "For friendship."

9 Afternoon. While coming back into the hotel, the giant from Nielele threw himself into me to crush me with his muscular mass. And he would have done it if heroic Jean had not shouldered in between us, holding him back for two seconds which was enough to bring the police force, in the form of the shady doorman dressed like an American policeman, and then the other vendors springing into action, getting into the fray with the gendarme. But I wasn't thinking of warring with human brothers, I wanted a Socratic dialogue with the indigenous man who had tangled with me. That is why I held the giant in an arm-lock, taking him away from the threat of the policeman and pulling him into the hotel lounge. He was in enemy territory there, in sight of and being watched by the hangers-on at the reception desk; I was thinking, therefore, that with my dialectics I could make him confess having sold me a knickknack for twice its worth. This is what I had accused him of on the street, provoking his sudden outburst of rage. But dialectics and enemy territory did not make the giant of Nielele back off one bit; he demolished Socratic dialogue with the more nimble sophist arts: "They told me that it's only worth 10,000 CFA." "Because they're jealous, don't you understand that there's envy and jealousy." "But you picked a fight with me." "I have a family that doesn't eat if I don't go back with that money, what do you think?" "I don't trust you anymore." "But your friend trusts me, true? doesn't he trust me?" He had the invincible patience of a walker in the savanna. And in his dignified boubou, the body of a heavy-middleweight fighter, the proud face that conceded nothing, he seemed to me like a warrior-leader reduced to selling knickknacks, but one with a great past. He has even been in Italy, tested his mettle. He comes on foot every day to sell something, with his suitcase of necklaces and bracelets, from the village of Nielele or from one with a similar name.

10 This evening an encounter with the hotel's prostitute, a young woman who made me think I was seeing things. For three-quarters of the conversation, I thought that she was a chemistry professor, that's the idea I had, even though she also seemed to me to have some Indian in her. She had the mannerisms of a scientist, the speech of an educated French woman, the refined face and dress of an exotic bourgeois, plus professorial eyeglasses. I had thought that she was in the white ghetto as a scientist who had come for a conference. And I continued with that idea even when I found her strangely insistent on the notion that we spend the evening together . . .

11 Morning. We're in a pirogue on the Senegal River, with three Wolof boys and a couple who are French tourists. River a kilometer wide, the sky streaked with formations of pelicans who tend to fly in threes, with the one at the top of the triangle acting as pilot. Our guide is named Mandou Sow, a skinny boy about eighteen years old, who has been in Italy and wears American Marine boots purchased in Trento. Coming here, he seemed happy to be in charge of us; at the market he bought supplies, very efficiently. On open road in the savanna, various baboons watched us closely, at first immobile, then making lopsided jumps. Farther on, dromedaries roaming freely, bushes of Indian figs, palm trees, limpid sky but invaded by red sand suspended in air.

12 We're passing in front of a fishing village. Many pirogues on the beach overrun with garbage. Masses of birds fluttering around a boat that is returning from fishing. Other birds are perched on the worn-out wreckage of a concrete pier. Cormorants fly shrieking with elongated silhouettes, other birds which perhaps are kingfishers dive perpendicularly underwater for fish . . . We're in front of a large island covered with birds shrieking all together with great enthusiasm, pelicans, cormorants, petrels, little egrets, others. As the pirogue approaches, the petrels surround us, and now we're going toward a spit of sand where I see a huge number of pelicans clustered together. Frankly, it seems to me I've found myself in the middle of a wildlife documentary, but neither I nor Ridolfi will rule out nature, trees, birds . . .

13 The extreme tip of the Langue de Barbarie peninsula. There in front, the huge surge of the ocean, and behind, the calm water of the Senegal River. Incredibly light sand, white at certain points. In the middle area, gathered by wind on the crest of a low dune, shells and plastic sacks: two nearly inde-structible things that will survive all the storms of the world. These two types of discards carried by ocean waves and waves of tourists, in far-off centuries to come will make up a fossil mu-seum. What will also exist will be the masses of yellow crabs, the swarms of egrets, but perhaps the so-called man who invented plastic sacks will survive only as an image in an exhibit . . . On the shore, populations of yellow crabs with eyes like vibrating hat pins. All of them very gentlemanly, rather timid, grouped to-gether in clans or tribes, maybe each one with a particular social position. They too will have their customs, their timetables, their quarrels, their loves, maybe even civic hatred against those who do not adhere to official values. Passing by, I saw how pelicans shriek: they throw open their long beaks, and the sack hanging beneath the beak expands to become a wind-vane, flat and as large as a tennis racket. They are extraordinarily piercing cries, as if the birds are fighting for a centimeter of space, like some people who are always in groups but can't stand the others.

14 The trip around the point done, quick stop, we get off at a fishing village. A dog wanders on the beach, sniffing through the garbage, a girl washes pans in the dirty river water. One hun-dred meters from the shore, two huts with straw roofs, in the open space a large straw canopy. Here on the left an open arcade made of falling-down plaster, where a boy is cooking fish. On the right, some men hammering a great iron cube which one might say was an old container, perhaps being adapted for other uses with the usual makeshift African know-how. Uninterrupted twittering coming from the little girls behind me, drowned out only by the hammering to take apart the container. Around the fish that is being cooked some boys are smoking marijuana, furnished by the guide of the two Frenchmen, a pleasure-seeking type who has to be in the center of things, named Bassirou . . . I don't know why we have come here by pirogue to these places, because we let ourselves be convinced by the boy Mandou. But this must be an obligatory trip in the life of a tourist, empty moments when he doesn't know what to do with himself. Humbly, we too will embrace this ritual because of the simple fact that the airplane ticket does not provide for an immediate return trip home.

15 Jean annoys me when he is a know-it-all, and most of all when he is a know-it-all about Paris. But at the moment, Jean finds himself faced with one who is much more of a know-it-all about Paris than he is. It's the other guide, the pleasure-seeking, center-of-attention-loving Bassirou, who lived in Paris for many years; he brags that he adored it there, that he had many women, danced every evening, didn't do anything, made a lot of money, that is to say sold drugs. The men around the container being taken apart have not stopped their hammering, my ears are ringing, it's very hot. We have eaten under the straw canopy, everyone around a tray with two huge groupers cooked with onions, or perhaps it was the Nile perch we always eat. Bassirou ate more than anyone, he has no scruples about it, while his two French customers eat little. Our guide, Mandou, only picked at his food, perhaps intimidated by braggart Bassirou who has been talking nonstop for an hour . . . Mandou is very downhearted, and he pulls me aside to explain that the money for the meal has all come from him. Bassirou has taken him under his wing as the elder guide but has not come up with a dime for his customers' provisions.

16 The two French people, husband and wife, come from a town near Sète, are traveling like we are with local means of transportation and without a goal. I'm happy to talk with them. My precautions against other tourists have been dismantled since I started thinking that each tourist goes to the same places that others who are a little similar to him go, just so he doesn't feel too out of place (for which reason it is not the fault of the others if he feels out of place in certain places). Waiting to go back, Jean sent a little boy over to me to climb up a very tall palm and throw down coconuts to us. There is a fixed price for this service, and the boy summoned as a specialist has a special uniform for doing it. Now he's gone to change and comes back with different pants and shirt . . . The ones with the container to break apart have finished their work and all of them are sleeping, deliciously, lying on the sheets of iron. The light begins to weaken, the water of the river sparkles, and I must talk about the village barber. A skinny, lanky fellow, with a shaved head, postmodernist sunglasses, a black tee shirt with white American words, DELIGHTFULLY TACKY YET UNREFINED, it is he who is the village's trend-setter. He has just finished cutting a customer's hair, with a simple razor blade, in the open arcade where they're cooking fish. Now, he's listening to the muezzin who's preaching loudly over the loudspeaker, but he listens to him while flipping through an advertising catalog.

17 The wait in the pirogue in the heat, extremely long. Wearisome discussion with the young Mandou, screwed by the expert Bassirou who cows him and has already left without paying. Mandou would like us to pay for the other tourists who have eaten without a single contribution to Bassirou, otherwise he will be out the money he should have made. I come up with thoughts that are not particularly edifying, they would deflate even the celebrated writer who looked for political inspiration in the Third World. The white man is a mammal destined for incessant assault by small black maenads, but often wants to believe himself to be a just and charitable man, just so he can put himself above this nemesis of distributive justice. Useless thoughts, I'll leave it to the writer with a great social commitment, who explains Africa with infinite paternalism by dint of generalized concepts. We're ready to leave, the pirogue is docked. I will remember the village that extends here behind us, it's called Tassinère, extending from a winding street—women at the doors, the old people on benches, the girls on walks to make themselves seen, the boys and young men on the hunt for something, life as it usually is at this hour of the day.

18 Morning. Jean is awake, has gone out of the hut with a nude torso, with the jogging pants he uses as pajamas. Then he started to stretch, looking at the river. Immediately, the young guide started in on us to get the money not agreed upon. But since Jean was demoted as our leader yesterday, he sent him back to me. I sent the young guide back to St. Louis, with a sendoff of 10,000 CFA to get him out of our hair. So, finally, we are without a guide, without a governess, without the hangers-on in the hotel who want to help us out. The owner of the hut, Mr. Pené, is very pleased we are here to eat and drink under his direction. He is the leather craftsman in the village behind here, and the nearest little town has the Anglo name Richard Toll. I continue to read René Caillé's *Journey to Timbuktu,* and Jean, on the sand, reads a book about the origins of the universe, while Mr. Pené has gone to buy bread and jam for us. Some girls from the neighborhood have already come to contemplate us. Some boys approach us saying: "Bonjour, ça va?" All the rituals are respectful, but when they see us reading, they don't disturb us.

19 The majority of the fishing village is on the other side of an inlet more to the south, where you see many pirogues. Here there are only two, which are broken down. The river's water is very dirty, the sky is still a bit cloudy, whitish. Here too, many cormorants that fly in extended silhouettes, shrieking. Here too, there is someone hammering something made of iron, behind us. Farther on, children are throwing stones at birds.

Goats and chickens wander around in search of something to eat because domesticated animals have to provide for their own needs, they're not kept like ours. I'm also seeing a terribly thin cat, like all the cats here, who have a less entitled look than ours when they take a nap.

20 Mr. Pené has four sons, three daughters. He worked in the Bata shoe factory in Dakar, now closed, and he came back to the village with his wife eight years ago, putting himself to work as a leather craftsman. His ancestors up until his great-grandfather lived in Mauritania and farmed the oasis in the service of the Maurs, certainly as slaves. Mr. Pené keeps us a long time, talking to us about the war between Mauritania and Senegal a few years ago, to tell us with precision that the Maurs are racists and do not want to recognize the rights of blacks. Mrs. Pené looks at her husband with a certain admiration when he gets stirred up and speaks in French. The children are not interested in these discussions in front of their parents' hut, where we have eaten dinner, but they are very interested in Jean's watch, a Walt Disney travel watch. The youngest son goes to school five kilometers from here. The oldest son, eighteen, goes to St. Louis to sell the leather worked by his father. He tried life in Dakar, but he got out because he couldn't make it there. He wants to go to Italy, following certain friends who are settled in parts of Reggio Emilia in agricultural jobs. Mr. Pené is religious, but he doesn't care for the marabout of the place because he says he steals from the houses. Even the muezzin who sings at five seems to annoy him, as he does us, because he has a hoarse voice that chokes each time he invokes Allah. The poor muezzin here doesn't have a microphone, so as a result he maybe has lost his voice by forcing it in order to make himself heard. Mrs. Pené is always quiet. I don't know where the daughters have gone.

21 We're reading a lot, taking long walks and talking about Spinoza's philosophy. As we walked in the savanna and saw some baboons, I succeeded in applying Spinoza to the tourist question as well. Jean got the idea of making a documentary on the life of tourists. We ruminated on the fact that anthropologists don't have much work to do anymore with primitive populations, which have been reduced to impoverished exiles or exotic appearances. A few rare teams follow the last groups in the Amazon forests, but if they find them still nude, with bow and arrow, they immediately contaminate them with colds or flu, illnesses that are lethal for them. So therefore, why not put an end to it and select a subject that is less perishable, which is exactly what tourists are? Tourists are healthy, almost all of them speak English, they're a group of people sharply on the rise. On top of that, they have already worked out their own belief system, a very complex mythology, their own customs of dressing and eating and traveling. The important thing, Jean says, is that at this point they are a true people. And so here we suddenly have a fraternal love for all tourists, because perhaps they are the only people whom one can be part of at this point, either as perpetual travelers or as drifters.

22 The reading of Caillé's *Journey to Timbuktu* gives me no peace, and all the places around here are alive with spirits, because he (René Caillé) came from St. Louis to this area in 1832, passing himself off as a renegade who wanted to become a Muslim, living among the nomadic Berbers, above all on Muslim charity. To read a book in the places he speaks of makes everything legendary. But even more so here because there are no tour markers, we're vague on it and we can't find ourselves even on Jean's small map . . . Yesterday, discussion with an ancient, slightly cross-eyed gentleman, who claimed he had seen me before. I asked if he had seen me in St. Louis. No, he saw me there in the village about five years ago. So then I wanted to know if by any chance he had seen my spirit outside me, you never know, because the spirit travels. He said: "I see your spirit well, my friend." "What does it look like?" "Little color, it moves around too much." Then he started back up along the main road.

23 People here are not particularly morning people. The hut behind us starts stirring only around nine. Then people circulate, taking a walk, cleaning their teeth, while they listen to an incessant radio that plays African reggae. Farther along, the path is strewn with garbage in the sand, there are six palm trees, all of them distorted toward the right. Up there about eight, they start to transport carts pulled by small asses, sometimes an entire family on the carriage goes to the city. At the edges of the village, on the main road, about nine, women with loads on their heads arrive and squat down to sell their wares. The men stand around chatting, and in the morning I often notice their art of spitting in long streams, a national art that results from the dust that is always in the mouth. Someone in the booths starts pulling out merchandise from a sack, but slowly, slowly. Displayed along the road are wicker baskets, beautiful large baskets made with different designs, plus brooms, detergents, buckets and plastic receptacles, stocks of plastic bags, vegetables, bananas, coconuts, onions. Then the women fish-sellers arrive, who sit on the ground with a display of big fish in baskets. In this part of the main street, there's a house with a courtyard enclosed by four disassembled automobile bodies placed on their side, which form an ingenious low wall, in addition to being yet another example of makeshift handiwork. Still farther behind, the houses have the courtyard protected by the wall, and the comings and goings are more intense than elsewhere. About nine, women with babies hanging on their backs come out carrying a basin of laundry, others sweep the floor of the house with precision, others line up at a pump to fill the basins. An old woman with a rubber hose distributes the water, the others give her a coin in payment. Life flowing along affects me, especially in the morning. Yesterday morning as soon as I woke up, I heard an ass who was farting, with mild sounds, almost sweet.

24 Afternoon. After a walk with backpacks along the main road and a lift from a driver as far as Richard Toll, we're now headed toward Mauritania. We're in a car with a Wolof driver who does not speak French. We can't agree about anything. Five minutes in Richard Toll, and a clinging sponger is found. Not even names are of use in making yourself understood with this unsociable man. He seems put out, maybe he doesn't like being alone with two whites. Marshes, a road full of holes, flat horizon, many shells in the sand, pelicans, border, we are almost at the Djamà Dam . . . Our last evening with Mr. and Mrs. Pené we had a pleasant dinner in the open air. In the morning a girl poked her head into our hut, I don't know who she was, then she ran off. In and out of cities, villages, families, ponds, we are always like fish getting away, like migratory birds who have gotten off course. Jean nods off in the car and does not listen to my reflections.

25 Border problem: the unsociable one does not want to go into Mauritania. The dam at Djamà is a long bridge, with huge cubical forms in the middle of the road, Senegal is on this side of the border, Mauritania on the other. Halted on the Senegalese side; a square, shabby structure is the customs house. Border gate, shit on the ground, two children with an ass, three old people underneath a tree, the unsociable one sulking in the car. The customs officer, a tall and gangly gentleman, seems like a retired humanist in the receiving area of his office. He likes to converse, he is well informed about African cinema today, but about the old French cinema as well, and we find ourselves in agreement in our admiration for the great Louis Jouvet. We talk about Jean's documentary on Mauritania, an idea that came to me right then and there, and the gentlemanly customs officer seems interested in the project. Then he searches everywhere for a piece of paper to write a brief note to his Mauritanian colleague. Drawers full of sheets of paper, but he can't find an unused one in the entire office. I give him one. Then he gets down to work with beautiful flowery handwriting, from another time, like my father's. He slowly moves his hand: "Dear colleague . . ." Now he's trying to persuade our unsociable one in the car. He urges us to remember his name, Kamou, if we need something . . .

26 Same scene, Mauritanian border. The unsociable one comes to a halt, he does not want to go into Mauritania. Now it comes out that he has no papers, no passport, nothing. The Mauritanian official, kind and severe, tries to convince him with the patience of a saint. That other one has no papers and answers crossly. Hearing the story of the locations for a documentary (invented in the office of Mr. Kamou, to which Kamou referred in the note), the official agrees to give the unsociable one a pass as far as Rosso, where he must present himself to the police . . . Here there are two square, shabby structures, one is the customs house. It is an unpaved road. Goats lying in the shade, an ass flicking its tail hard. Men under a scrawny little tree smile at us. A black woman crouching down nurses a baby. Behind customs, clothes hang out to dry on a line. Pearl-gray sky with deep blue openings. The official has a lot to do, they have called him into the office. An enormous black car arrives filled with black people dressed for a party. It seems like they're going to a wedding or coming back from something of that nature. All around in the open space, marshes and desert, in places, steppe with strange red lichen. It's already the sun of the sunset.

27 Eight or ten kilometers into Mauritania, on the path toward Rosso, the sullen one does not want to go any farther. He has already stopped almost every kilometer; he really cannot stand Mauritania. We would have already arrived in Rosso, if he hadn't kept digging his heels in; we would have already sent him back home with the ferry. But it's impossible to understand one another, even with my mimetic talents. He shrugs his shoulders when I tell him off. Today I have to be the leader, Jean has handed in his resignation. Impossible to have a discussion with him, he sits there sulking. While Jean seems absent, we wait in silence. In the middle of this desert we truly are phantoms of tourists, like the phantoms the exorcist of Brighton talked about, faint spirits that can't find their way.

28 Morning, turning back, after various adventures. At the border between Mauritania and Senegal one has the impression that the world changes. One comes from a country made of sand, with isolated peaks that are crumbling in the wind, and one moves toward the fertile areas of Senegal. Here the savanna is an arid terrain with very few trees, interrupted by scattered swamps or the remains of swamps from the rainy season, which now are coated white with salt. Wandering around, you don't see birds, which spring out in masses once you're barely back in Senegal. Bleak land in the final strip of Mauritania: there is nothing special to see, one can only grant it the extraordinariness that the world of absence and emptiness gives, the optimal place for contemplation. A few kilometers from the border, we see groups of black women who walk along with huge loads on their heads, very happy, they wave to us laughing. Signs that we have entered a more populated world, more animated, more colorful, because black Africa begins here. The Mauritanians on the other hand, Maurs or Moors, are fierce adversaries of blackness, aside from the fact that they still have black slaves or ex-slaves cultivating the land because they are nomadic merchants. We learned this and other things from the French merchant met along the way in Mauritania, who took us back to St. Louis. He says that with the Maurs, one can speak in Arabic, in French, in a lingua franca called Poulaar, but not in Wolof, language of the black slaves. A Moorish merchant would not lower himself by dealing in that language.

29 After three days in Mauritania looking around, almost without hearing anyone speak, it's very striking to find ourselves under the tent of this French merchant, who is Muslim, named Michel Grandet and called Ishmael, who picked us up on the street. He's from Montpellier, but when we talked to him about Montpellier, it seemed to me he changed the subject twice. Blond, with a long ponytail, he's about thirty, married in St. Louis to a Wolof woman. He studies the Koran and is an avid reader of books. We were sitting cross-legged on the rugs of his Moorish tent, constructed like one from a circus, hanging down from a central pole. He said that the Maurs don't keep hold of anything, they're nomads, they throw away everything. The only things they keep are jewels to offer women in matrimony, and he goes to Mauritania to buy them and then sell them to tourists in St. Louis. He showed us necklaces and Moorish jewels, telling many stories about each one. The necklaces in multicolored glass, *chevronné,* that comes from Venice, are made with granules from Murano that come from the 1500s. The ones with amazonite and other opaque stones, unknown to me, come from Asia Minor, some actually from the Sumerians. He showed us a huge book where all the Moorish jewels are catalogued, along with their places of origin. But it had the effect of a dream, finding ourselves talking with someone from Montpellier under a tent in the desert, with two black watchmen outside posted as sentinels. This evening, after having gone to see him in his beautiful house, with balconies that look out at St. Louis, flowers and plants on the terrace, everything truly exotic, we asked ourselves what has brought him here. He has said that we can write to him at the Hôtel Résidence, the best place to reach him, because he is a friend of the owner. He became a Muslim, married a Wolof woman, studies the Koran, but his most secure reference point is still the white ghetto, as it is for us tourists.

NINTH NOTEBOOK

1 Comfortable return trip to Dakar with our own car and driver. Crossing the countryside, along the way, the driver stops to make purchases and deliver letters. Arriving in a village, he says to the first person who happens along: "This is for so-and-so of such-and-such." He's a kind of courier who competes with the post office. Butchers along the street, in leather aprons, in their booths made of straw, with half an ox hanging and covered with flies. They all have smiling faces that bring to mind beefsteaks. A woman with an emerald-green dress arrives, another one with a full and fluttering yellow dress, a turban of white organza. All this elegance in open countryside leaves me bewildered and allured . . . The bare savanna, birds, tamarisks, shepherd-children with cows. Stopped at a roadblock, a police-man with a machine gun. The driver says that these roadblocks are the result of the confusion in the Casamance . . . A village of huts enclosed by a stockade made of cane, over which cloth has been spread out, a spectacle in Technicolor. Just like colors, words, in the same way, cannot be drab, uncertain, they must be vivid, blaring, or else it's better to remain quiet. The driver stops along the way to buy rice: lively discussion with the vendor seated on a sack, who every once in a while spits out one of those long-streamed spits, which serves as a pause in the bargaining. Then we give a ride to a distinguished gentleman with white scarf and umbrella, who must go to Thiès . . . At Rufisque, about noon, children playing soccer with a minuscule ball. At the first red light in Dakar, a vendor selling sheets from the Koran comes up, but at the same time a skeletal little boy starts cleaning the car's windshield. The furious driver gets out to chase him away, and he screams at him even as he's running away. Then, coming to the area near the bus station, he has a nervous breakdown over the deadly traffic. He gets out of the car, unbuttons his shirt, spits at the ground, looks for a taxi and pays for it to take us to the hotel. He says he just can't manage crossing through Dakar. He entrusts us to a young man with a shaved head, with a gruesome expression, who, first thing, asks us if we're Americans.

2 Landed at the Hôtel Nina, much more modest but not much different from the Sofitel in terms of atmosphere. I have a textbook case of African tourism to write down. This afternoon I went to have a sandwich on the Avenue Pompidou, and as I was eating, prostitutes who were little girls approached me. There were four of them, between the ages of ten and fourteen. They touched me, they put their hands on my shoulders, I brusquely sent them away. But they didn't get upset by this, no, they even showed how well they understood me. Rolling their shoulders way back to display their breasts, they went in search of other customers until the waiter sent them out of the bar. A little while later at the Hôtel Nina, I found some guy in the lobby who was holding an Italian newspaper. He was a cloth dealer from Modena, who traded on the markets, a short plump guy, a bit bald, a wide, nice face. He was talking to Jean, and he said that winter is the dead season in his business, so every winter he travels the world in order to go to bed with black prostitutes. With a meek and modest tone, he explained that he has gone everywhere, each year to a different country, always with that goal, for fifteen years. He complained that the one from the other night had stolen 20,000 CFA from him while he was getting dressed. "They're sharp, they're born with that instinct." However, he was still under the spell of the body of the thief, her long legs. Then he expounded upon the differences between black prostitutes in Kenya, Gabon, the Ivory Coast, Brazil, Madagascar. According to him, the young prostitutes of Madagascar blush when it's time to go to bed: "They're timid, they're tender, it's necessary to go slowly with them, you know! To tell you the truth, I left my heart there with them." It seemed like a romantic tale. Then, however, came his wistful confession, made to Jean, leaning down in his armchair: "There's AIDS, I always use a condom, but you know! I'm fifty-nine years old, maybe I have ten years left, and I'll go on as long as I'm able." At this point the prostitutes from the Avenue Pompidou cheerily entered the lobby, smothering his bald head with kisses, hugging him and calling him "uncle." He was reluctant, but also a bit consoled by that outpouring. He kept his eyes lowered. One of the ones from the reception desk came over to chase away the little girls, who were making too much of a disturbance.

3 Houses, clothes, means of transportation, merchandise, shops, streets: I tried to remember the objects that are new that I've seen on these journeys. I have seen almost nothing that's new, everything shows the signs of age, everything broken and mended as well as possible. Even new things have the outmoded appearance of war surplus. All means of transportation are left-overs from other times, for example, these buses, TRANS-PORT EN COMMUN, that one sees in Dakar, colored, broken-down remnants, packed with people. All the clothes are traditional, or else discards from our world. Almost all the shops are dark caverns, where the merchandise seems like remnants recovered from who knows where. Even the new shops down-town have a look of incipient disrepair. The poster of Madonna, faded from the sun as well, seems like it comes from a distant past. And the barbers' signs, which show haircuts in style in American ghettos, make me think of archeological finds of an America that passed out of style decades ago already . . . Observations that are little different, on the road going to Dakar. In the country, in the morning, one sees these women who are going shopping, waiting for a bus, are selling something, but they always have clothing that looks new and expensive, ironed, never crumpled, well adjusted around their bodies, the cloth that falls well, even with wearing a strap tied around the waist to carry babies on backs. They walk with those radiant colors against black skin, one can tell that making a good impression is important to them, even as everything around them is undone and dusty. I have seen women, to my eye amazingly elegant, crouched down beside piles of garbage, waiting for the bus, without this indifference to the foulness, unacceptable to us, seeming strange. I have also seen the insufferable Madonna among the trash, her face already washed out amid the scraps, with the heat that renders everything more perishable, no longer being redeemed by an advertising radiance.

4 We leave tomorrow. Jean is a little sick. We're going to have dinner in a restaurant that is one big room, where I like the fluctuating confusion of everything, with people of all kinds and races, waiters and waitresses who are always making mistakes, ordering three times from a menu where you don't understand anything. Here, absolutely nothing seems under control, and I would gladly come here to eat every evening if I were to stay in Dakar. Upon our return to the hotel, I find a pack of matches with the image of a cowboy hat, with the caption: "Un pas de plus vers l'Ouest." It's the Marlboro slogan, which points to the west as the direction of the march of progress. "Another step toward the West." But will the Africans go toward the west? Will they become nervous, depressed, maniacal for having everything under control? Will they believe in privacy, vacations, projects, focused on the future and never on the present? Will they become ashamed of the perishability of bodies, of old stuff, of discards, of makeshift things, of mended objects? Will they do away with the natural disorder of things, illegal contact of bodies, the mixing together of new and old, of the fresh and the putrid? Nighttime meditations in Dakar . . .

5 Appointment with Batouly at the Café de Paris, she with sore teeth, unhappy that we are leaving. Difficult conversation. She has a furious outburst, saying that she detests Dakar: "Do you think I like living here?" She wants to escape to Paris, but now she cannot because of her children. We go with her to her house to say good-bye to the Sarr family. Then at the house, she shows us the photos of beautiful dresses she has worn on the important occasions of her life. A passion for clothing like the Italians', like my mother's. Few other photos have importance, except for those of their father, the jewel of the family (and the one above the bed, where there is her father with the Emperor Haile Selassie.) She also puts a great deal of importance on the pictures that show the law office where she works, because she's happy there. She feels protected there, as she does with her dresses, it seems to me. Today, instead, she had dressed in mourning clothes, casually for the first time, in European clothing. She supports the family, her ex-husband does not give money for the children, her sister doesn't find work, getting downtown is truly problematic in Dakar. In the five minutes in that small room, apart from when she said those phrases, I saw her go completely to pieces, as if she had an arm on the dresser, a leg on the bed, her head on the floor. I wanted to touch her fingers remaining up in the air, to say affectionate things, but it's useless to utter our senseless phrases. Away from it all, the taxi waited; when I play the good man, it is the falsest performance.

6 At the Dakar airport, there is no way to sit down, except on the rim of a flower box. But there, every minute someone came by to accost us. A plane from Brussels was due to arrive, and in the terminal there were kids circulating everywhere waiting to assault the tourists. There were all kinds of them: the ones sent by hotels and tourist agencies, the overgrown adolescents with rock-star sunglasses, the hunters of Americans in flashy clothes, the guides who are expert in snaring the stragglers, and the carnival hucksters with junk to sell. You could tell which category of tourists they would set their sights on from the way they were dressed or the way they carried themselves. The only one we weren't able to classify was one with a torn tee shirt, who circulated around the airport holding a big fish attached to a hook. He didn't want to sell his fish, he carried it around as if it were a banner. When the plane from Brussels arrived later, all the kids waiting could no longer hold themselves back. From the balcony, they scrutinized the rosy Germans, the pale Belgians, who got off the plane unaware of what awaited them. Jean, excited as well, pointed out the scene to me. You breathed in an exalted air of big game hunting on the international arrivals floor. As soon as the tourists passed through customs, the assault was unleashed, and it was a sight never to be forgotten. Theater of audacious moves, with a flavor of the rabble at fairs of past times, it seemed more interesting to me than our playbill comedies.

7 Dakar-Bamako, evening flight. Night at the Bamako airport, where we got off and now have to wait for the plane to Paris, which will arrive at 4:30. There's no place to sit except on these uncomfortable metal chairs, extremely narrow, in the dark of the big waiting area. My ill pal is unable to stand and he has gone into the *salon payant,* where paying for entry gives one the right to sit in an armchair. One also has the right to drink a Coca-Cola and make conversation with two rich men, in Western dress, but very black, with colored handkerchiefs poking out of their coats' breast pockets. Here, instead, others sleep on the floor and snore beautifully. . . The last textbook case of African tourism to record before leaving. Yesterday morning in the Hôtel Nina, in the lobby, I heard the conversation of a bony American with a Senegalese travel agent. The agent was supposed to bring her to a ceremony with masks in a coastal village. They discussed the prices, and the Senegalese proposed taking her to see the warriors' dances as well, with the special tourist rate. At this point the bony American declared that she was a professor of art in a college, and that she was interested strictly in African masks. The Senegalese looked around, he listened, annoyed. Then the American declared herself to be an artist as well and, from her bag, pulled out an album of photographs of her paintings, explaining that, in these paintings, she paints only African masks, because she does Theme Art. The Senegalese looked at the photos, he listened, annoyed. He straightened up only when she asked him if there was an artisan capable of designing African frames for her. Since she did Theme Art, the frame had to be in keeping with the theme of the African masks, you understand. The Senegalese looked at her a bit perplexed, perhaps because frame-making is a European craft, not African. But the other demonstrated virginal trust, that pure lack of doubt that is like a spell in a fairy tale. And she insisted that she could only use an African type of frame for her paintings of African masks in her next exposition in America, but that it had to be "truly African." Definitive frame, truly African, for Americans.

8 I had thought I had ended the journal, but the airplane was delayed. We crossed through the police office because our visas had expired. The official on duty seemed to be imitating detectives from American movies, with the holster under his armpit. The attendant from the *salon payant* accompanied us, having put himself in the position of interceding for us, given that we had paid, we were under his protection, part of the family . . . Now, in the waiting room, I think of a Muslim cemetery that we saw the day before yesterday. Below that low promontory, between tombs made of small blocks of naked stone, without names and without words, there was the idea of a way of dying that is completely silent and without laments. Small white stones, the only funereal sign, scattered haphazardly on the slope. A depository of anonymous earthlings. Jean said that death is not emotionally moving, it's life that moves us. Death is like a chemical agent that gives color to life. The anonymous tombs, a migrating cormorant, strange tires planted in the sand, some sheep grazing, and the guy who was guiding us with a tired demeanor: here are the last images I wrote down in my journal.

Then the overcast sky, the first drops of rain we have seen on this trip: huge drops, long and thin, immediately absorbed by the clay of a low crumbling wall.

9 On the airplane coming from Dakar, they showed us a tourism documentary on Senegal. It showed the multicolored markets, the usual female vendors, the usual carts pulled by asses, the usual villages of the savanna, the cormorants, the pelicans. It was the documentary of the places where we had been. Jean, half-serious, said: "We've been in the middle of a tourist documentary . . ." Yes, however, getting off in Europe, here too, it's like being in a perpetual documentary, where you see everything clean, orderly, smooth, glossy, flashing, redone, not even one discard in sight, not a car falling to pieces, no dress truly out of fashion, a store that's like it was five years ago, a window display with books that are not absolutely new. We wander around Paris and we see only this other documentary of total newness, with there no longer being anything precarious, poor, falling apart, patched together, worm-eaten by the wind, rejected by destiny. It is the documentary on global simulation, without place, without escape, which they show us in the headlines of ads day and night, behind the protective glass we are equipped with in order to live in these places. But then one knows that when one is left behind a window, he tends to feel that he's missing something, even if he has everything and he's wanting for nothing, and this lack of nothing perhaps counts for something, because one can also be aware of not needing anything at all, except some of the nothing he truly lacks, some of the nothing that cannot be bought, some of the nothing that does not correspond with anything, the nothing of the sky and the universe, or the nothing that the others have who do not have anything.